D0015623

get married this year

get

365 Days to "I Do"

married
this year

Janet Blair Page, PhD

Creator of the acclaimed "I Will Be Married in a Year" course

Avon, Massachusetts

Published by
Adams Media, a division of F+W Media, Inc.
57 Littlefield Street, Avon, MA 02322. U.S.A.
www.adamsmedia.com

ISBN 10: 1-4405-2206-5
ISBN 13: 978-1-4405-2206-2
eISBN 10: 1-4405-2779-2
eISBN 13: 978-1-4405-2779-1

Printed in the United States of America.

10 9 8 7 6 5 4 3 2 1

Library of Congress Cataloging-in-Publication Data
is available from the publisher.

This publication is designed to provide accurate and authoritative information with
regard to the subject matter covered. It is sold with the understanding that the publisher
is not engaged in rendering legal, accounting, or other professional advice. If legal
advice or other expert assistance is required, the services of a competent professional
person should be sought.
—From a *Declaration of Principles* jointly adopted by a Committee of the American
Bar Association and a Committee of Publishers and Associations

Many of the designations used by manufacturers and sellers to distinguish their
product are claimed as trademarks. Where those designations appear in this book and
Adams Media was aware of a trademark claim, the designations have been printed
with initial capital letters.

This book is available at quantity discounts for bulk purchases.
For information, please call 1-800-289-0963.

Dedication

Dedicated to my clients and students. It is their successes that have fueled and inspired my desire to write *Get Married This Year* in order to help many more women find their dream mate.

Acknowledgments

My deeply loved daughters Tasha and Liz and sons-in law Eric and Ian have been my idea people, critics, supporters, and fans. Mary Beth Chappell, my agent at Zachary, Shuster, and Harmsworth, has been extraordinarily generous with her time and caring and has been indispensable to creating and finishing the book. My mom, brother, sister-in-law, and the friends who are family to me have indefatigably been asking me how the book is going for years, have always cared about the answer, and provided continual support. Special thanks to Jim Black, Dr. Len Buccellato, Ken Spooner, Marie Masters, and Dr. Cedric Suzman for their guidance and for keeping me on track and to Mary Cobb Bugg Callahan, founder of Evening at Emory and creator of the class concept.

Contents

Introduction

After having some difficulty drawing her out in conversation, Sarah's date told her that she reminded him of tofu: no personality unless you flavored it. He said he meant to be funny. Sarah reported him to their single's matching service.

Vickie was excited to go on a blind date set up by mutual friends, but halfway through the first latte, she made her dating requirements very clear. She expected flowers at least twice a week, phone calls twice a day, and on weekends she intended to spend Friday through Sunday at his place. Her date decided not to take the job offer.

Mary Jo wanted a connected and committed relationship, but tended to unload every problem, neurosis, and life disadvantage she had onto a potential date the minute they met. The mere availability of an appealing man triggered her barrage of bad news—her spotty employment record, estranged dysfunctional family, and sometimes off the chart Adult Dysfunctional Disorder behaviors. What she saw as "putting everything out in the open right away," men saw (quite accurately) as her attempt to discourage them from asking her out.

In a misguided attempt at seduction, Amie stood in front of her lover naked and told him that he had better make it good because it sure hadn't been very satisfying the last time. His performance was limited.

Believe it or not: life really is stranger than fiction. These stories are real. I know because I've met the women involved in each and every one of them. Not surprisingly, the techniques described above had an abysmal success rate, which made the people using them feel like complete romantic failures. Now, behind such major bloopers—and even more minor ones—are almost always insecurity and a lot of anxiety that have to be dealt with. But with a little help—and some fear busting, dating skill building, and communication training—even these dating-challenged ladies got on track and found their perfect partners. And if *they* can do it, so can you.

How can I help you find your happily ever after? In 1984, I began teaching a course at Emory University in Atlanta called "Before a Year Is Over, I'll Be Married," and it was a hit from the very beginning. You may not realize it, but while the way people meet and date has changed drastically over the last three decades, the problems that women face in their relationships haven't changed at all; women still feel as though they're not meeting enough eligible people, or if they are, they keep facing the same relationship roadblocks over and over again. As a psychotherapist—divorced, widowed, and remarried myself—I'm not only able to empathize with many of these women, I've personally been on the same path, and have my own backlog of bloopers. But I've also experienced the joys of a good marriage, and it's the most wonderful way I can think of to spend a life. That said, you can trust me when I tell you that changing the way you think about and approach marriage is easier said than done. But my hope is that you can learn from the mistakes that my students, clients, and I have made before making your own. This book offers the depth of experience that I've gathered in the hopes that you will be able to use it to find a happy, healthy, and lasting relationship with the man of your dreams.

In the chapters to follow, you'll learn everything you need to know to become happy with yourself, to get your life ready for a lasting relationship, and to find, court, and keep a man. You'll learn how to meet eligible, commitment-worthy people who are both desirable and available, and you'll work to define what eligible and commitment-worthy actually mean for you. You'll also understand how to market yourself, become a smart "shopper," develop your action plan, and feel confident that you'll stay with your partner for the long run. This is a personal journey and a personal book; you'll have to do a lot of soul searching to figure out what you really want, need, and desire. As such, this is also a very interactive book so be sure to always have a pen or pencil handy. I encourage you to answer the questions on these pages; make notes, highlight, do whatever you need to do to get the most out of *Get Married This Year*—and yourself.

You'll notice that the marriage track described throughout the book is divided into twelve sections—each section represents a month. But you don't need to get married in a year, or thirteen months, or fourteen months. Simply getting "married off" isn't the goal here. Instead, focus on marrying well. The importance of setting a time frame for your goal is in direct relationship to your achieving it. This twelve-month deadline pushes you to make time in your life to meet, date, court, and mate. So start your work with the idea of getting married in a year, but don't worry if your time frame turns out to be longer or shorter. A great deal depends on where you already are in your search.

If you still think a deadline and time frame sound desperate or hurried, think about this: if you were looking for a job, you'd take the time to make sure your résumé was in order, you'd look terrific for the interview, and you'd be sure you had all the skills the company was looking for in great abundance. Finding a suitable mate may be the most important job search on which you'll ever embark, so you'll want to make sure your self-marketing skills are at their peak.

With all of the positive changes you'll be making to reach your goal, the coming year should be the best of your life (so far). In these twelve months, you have the opportunity to learn more about yourself and your relationships with others. The lessons you learn will be helpful in your future marriage, but you'll also reap the benefits in your work and friendships. Gather supporters around you; but please remember that you are your own best friend. The attitude you carry with you makes all the difference in the world, so congratulate yourself on every accomplishment. Your core challenge is to accept and embrace the necessity and excitement of a new beginning. And remember, love isn't simply a state of being or a feeling—love is an action verb. So start working and good luck!

One thing you know about your dating life is that what you are doing now isn't working. Pieces of it may be successful, but something about your attitude, self-confidence, self-awareness, time allocation, selection process, and/or social networking (online and in real life) leaves room for improvement. And self-improvement is just what you're going to learn in this chapter. Prepare yourself for a scrupulously honest assessment of yourself and what changes you need to make, your current happiness and satisfaction levels, interpersonal skills, and capacity for giving and receiving love in your life. Some of it may be hard, but if you're honest with yourself along the way, you'll be glad you decided to go along for the ride. The changes you choose to both make and act on will not only benefit you in all areas of your life, but will also ensure that with every step you take, you increase the probability of success in attracting a dream mate with similar capabilities to relate and love. Let's get started!

Chapter 1

Know Yourself

Myth: The right person will complete you.
Truth: The right person will be a good match for the person you are.

So, you want to find your Prince Charming, your soul mate, "the one"? Before you can find the best person for you, you have to find yourself. Now, you don't need to go on a walkabout through Australia, jump out of an airplane, or sell all of your belongings and commit to a year of minimalism, but you do need to truly know yourself, inside *and* out.

One thing you already know is that you don't want to be alone and yet you're still single. Why is that? Are you acting too much like a single lady? Sometimes women unwittingly become professional singles who almost make a career out of staying solo. Are you commitment phobic, afraid that by agreeing to a second or third date, you're "stuck" for life? Perhaps you're a fantasy chaser, deciding what song you'll dance to at your wedding before your first date has ended? These scenarios are serious roadblocks to relationship success. The good news is that with enough hard work, you can jump right over them into a lasting, committed relationship. You just need enough self-awareness to know if you're the one putting up these roadblocks in front of the very same destination that you're trying to reach.

Personal Data Form

When trying to get a clear picture of the way others see them, many women have found it informative to have their lives laid out in front of them in black and white. For our purposes, your answers will come in handy throughout the rest of this book—especially when analyzing your Spouse Shopping List in Chapter 2. Take all the time you need to openly and honestly fill out the Personal Data Form below. You're the only person who's going to see it, so don't be shy or hold anything back.

All About You

Age: _____

Occupation: _____

Education: _____

Annual income: _____

Number of children: _____

Gender, ages, and trials, tribulations, and joys of each child (if applicable): _____

_____

_____

_____

Your religious or spiritual background: _____

_____

Your current religious or spiritual beliefs, if any: _____

_____

Most significant person in your life and why: _____

_____

Who took primary care of you as an infant: _____

_____

Your experience with school: _____
_____

What did you like best when you were ten years old? _____
_____

Describe your health history: _____
_____
_____

Your current physical activity level: _____
_____

Have you ever thought you had a problem with alcohol, drugs, sex, food, or gambling? _____
_____

Your Family
Mother's occupation: _____
_____

Mother's age/cause of death (if applicable): _____
_____

Father's occupation: _____
_____

Father's age/cause of death (if applicable): _____
_____

Your parents' relationship status and quality: _____
_____

Number of brothers: _____
_____

Number of sisters: _____

_____

Your position in the family: _____

_____

Briefly describe your mother and father and how they were as parents:

- Mother: _____

  _____

- Father: _____

  _____

Other relatives who were especially important to you when you were growing up: _____

_____

Three words your family used to describe you when you were growing up: _____

_____

Briefly describe each sibling and your relationship with them: _____

_____

_____

_____

Did anyone in the family have a problem with alcohol, drugs, sex, food, or gambling? _____

_____

Was anyone disabled, mentally or physically? _____

_____

What would you most like to hear your parents say to you today?

_____

_____

Your Romantic History

Previous marriages: _____

_____

Previous serious relationships: _____

_____

Who were your loves, in chronological order? _____

_____

_____

What is the romantic "story" of each one ? _____

_____

_____

_____

_____

_____

If you could rewrite that story, how would it read? _____

_____

_____

_____

How would you like your romance story to end? _____

_____

_____

Your earliest memory of any kind: _____

_____

Your earliest sexual experience: _____

_____

Your earliest sexual intercourse: _____

_____

Your earliest orgasm: _____

_____

Your Life Today

Greatest sources of joy: _____

_____

Your goals, dreams, and wishes (all of them, including the ones you were discouraged from keeping): _____

_____

_____

_____

Present problem areas. Describe how the following areas are stressful:

- Work: _____

  _____

- Social: _____

  _____

- Children: _____

  _____

- Parents: _____

  _____

- Sexual: _____

  _____

- Other: _____

  _____

How do those stresses get in the way of having love in your life?

_____

_____

What are you going to do about it? _____

_____

_____

When are you going to get started? _____

_____

When you've finished filling out your Personal Data Form, read back through it. Do you think the facts you've written down on paper accurately represent you and the person you present to the world? This is your life up to this moment in time. The best favor you can do yourself is to accept who you are, and work to change the things you find you can't accept. After all, if you can't accept yourself, how do you expect anyone else to accept and respect you?

Identify Your Supporters

You can probably succeed in this twelve-month program on your own, but you are much better off with a village. You'll need people who can help you take breaks, to commiserate with and laugh off your failures, and to give you constructive feedback about how well you are staying on track. Even more importantly, the people who know you best will be able to tell you if you are presenting the real you to the new men you meet. Think about the people who are the most significant to you. It is this network of people you're going to need by your side as you begin this new journey. Surround yourself with those "family" members who love you, support you, are devoted to you, and vice versa.

If you've separated yourself from people who could be important, if there are things in your past that need repair or people who need forgiveness, now is the time to resolve these issues. Don't drag your unresolved problems forward. Rather than hiding from the truth, face it, and don't let it hold you back.

> **Love Notes**
>
> *Some friends and some family may be better as exes in your life or at least put on a very high and hard-to-reach shelf for the next year.*

The Story You Tell Yourself

Attitude really is everything. The difference between a positive and negative story can guarantee success or sink you. Comments like, "Men always leave me," "I'm not sure there are any happy marriages," or "I am only lovable until they know me," are major roadblocks to love. If you approach new experiences or new relationships with these kinds of comments in mind, you approach each new encounter with negativity. In this mood, you are a turnoff. Instead, approach dating with a personal story that says "Men usually like me and I like them," "Every date I go on is a great new possibility," or "I'll have a terrific time." With a positive attitude you bring a genuine and inviting smile with you—which is the most attractive thing you can wear on a date.

It's not always fun to realize what you're doing wrong. But once you realize that roadblock exists, and take the time to fix it, the result is a lot more fun than sitting around feeling lonely or complaining about being single. So, you're not perfect. Guess what? Nobody is. When you can forgive yourself for your mistakes, learn from them, and get past it, you'll find that you not only have an easier time dating, but that all of your relationships will become more pleasant and manageable.

LOVE STORIES: JO LYNN

Jo Lynn considered herself a very positive, funny person, and so did her friends. She was always laughing and joking, the real life-of-the-party type. But even with all her considerable entertainment skills, Jo Lynn couldn't get past the third date. She didn't understand why until she was out on a second date and her dinner companion commented that she complained a lot. While complaining about his remark to one of her friends, one of them pointed out that a complaint served with a smile is still a complaint. Turns out that what Jo Lynn thought of as lighthearted jokes were often at someone else's expense—and could easily be viewed as judgments. And any date knows, if only quasi-consciously, that sooner or later those criticisms will at some point be turned on him. It took a lot of practice and courage to break her bad habit, but once Jo Lynn was able to be completely positive through dates one and two, she got a lot more third, fourth, and fifth dates.

Reflect on your Recent History

For many, it's easy to tell a happy version of your life story; it can be a little harder to take a fresh look at your recent history. Take the time right now to reflect on the events of the last year by answering the following questions as they pertain to the past twelve months of your life.

- What did you do that you are not proud of? _____
  _____
- What were you most proud of? _____
  _____
- What gave you the most purpose? _____
  _____
- How did your ego get in the way? _____
  _____
- What was the funniest moment? _____
  _____
- What was your most embarrassing or humbling moment? _____
  _____
- What was your most romantic moment? _____
  _____
- What surprised you? _____
  _____
- Did you break any habits? _____
  _____
- If you could do anything over again, what would it be? _____
  _____
- Did somebody new come into your life? What does that person represent? _____
  _____
- Who and what are you most grateful for? _____
  _____
- What do you forgive yourself for? _____
  _____

You might need more room for that last question. In fact, right now, get out a piece of paper, write down everything you need to forgive yourself for, grant yourself forgiveness, and tear up that paper into tiny pieces. Then, either burn it, flush it, or throw it into a flowing river. It's a ritual that works. Confess, forgive, and let it go so you can move on. Your sense of deservedness depends on it. And your success in finding somebody truly great depends on believing you are wonderful enough to deserve him.

Your Love Résumé

When you imagine your dream job, you likely assess what you've chosen in the past in order to gain a better idea of what you need in the future. Now it's time for you to put the same care and preparation into your personal life and figure out what you want next by creating a Love Résumé. This trip down memory lane may not be completely pleasant, but cataloging your past relationships is a necessary step toward finding the one you can love and who loves you back. And hopefully you'll have some good memories to go along with the more painful ones.

Filling Out Your Love Résumé

So, how far back should your Love Résumé go? Forget the kid in the third grade who kissed you under the jungle gym, but if there was someone who really mattered to you and played a significant role in your life in high school or college, that person should be counted. Go with your own definition of love. As long as it's romantic love, it counts. Even if it was only a short relationship, feel free to add it on—especially if your dating pattern has been a series of short, intense relationships. If you had a two-week affair and consider that man the love of your life, who's to tell you that he's not? By all means, write it down.

To create your Love Résumé you'll need to do the following:

Column 1: Write the names of each of your loves.

Column 2: Physically describe all of your past loves. For each, write down the first three to six adjectives that pop into your head when you think about that person. For example: *"Peter: Tall, blond, bearded, snazzy dresser."* And don't panic; you're not going to be graded or judged. Just write down your quick, instinctual thoughts.

Column 3: List adjectives that describe your love relationships. Again, write down the first three to six descriptive words that come to mind. Was it fun? Volatile? Miserable? Romantic? Chaotic?

Column 4: Write down which one of you ended the relationships. And keep in mind that the answer may not be simple. Who was first to be forthcoming may be different from the one who started setting the relationship up to fail. Was it really you or your partner who threw in the towel? Again, no one else will see this, so check your ego at the door and write the truth.

Column 5: Take time and think about the personalities of each of your loves. Did their personality resemble either of your parents' personalities? If so, write that down.

SAMPLE LOVE RÉSUMÉ				
People you have loved	Their physical type	Adjectives that describe the relationship	Who ended it?	Did their personality resemble your mother or father?
Mike	Tall, handsome, dark hair, big eyes	Stormy, disagreed a lot	He left	Mother
Sam	Low on looks, small, sexy	Loving, nothing in common	Mutual	Father
Darrell	Heavy, great smile	Very sexual, different values	I left	Neither
Robert	Medium height, thin, sweet, open face	Tender, long distance	He left	Neither

YOUR LOVE RÉSUMÉ				
People you have loved	Their physical type	Adjectives that describe the relationship	Who ended it?	Did their personality resemble your mother or father?

Analyzing Your Résumé

Now that you've filled out your Love Résumé, look for patterns and themes. You'll recognize your past mistakes, particularly the repeated ones. Do you have a story that explains your making the same poor choices over and over? You need to start your new dating life knowing what you do and don't want to repeat. So what should you look for? Learn how to analyze your answers for each column below.

Love Notes

Doing the same thing over and over again, expecting a different outcome, may be one of the definitions of insanity.

Physical Type

You listed the physical characteristics of your past loves to check if you have a distinct physical type. If you have one or even a few types, you have a problem. Chances are that you, without even really thinking about it, are shopping only for that type and are eliminating other potential mates. When you have a type, you only really see people with those characteristics. You only see stunning blonds, buff bodies, or dark, brooding troubled men. If you go out looking for only a few types, the odds are already stacked against you.

Women like to believe that if they get exactly the type they want, it's an indicator that everything else will work out. But what you see isn't always what you get. The short, skinny guy might end up being the rock, or the less-than-good-looking man could be the best lover you could ever have imagined.

LOVE STORIES: RUBY

Ruby was a vivacious and independent woman who wanted a man who could protect her; someone who could safely and bravely get her out of a burning building. She wanted a burly guy with a firefighter's body and she wouldn't settle for anything else . . . until one eye-opening summer.

Ruby and her best girlfriend, Sally, were with a small team of volunteers helping at a camp in the mountains. Two other volunteers—Leonard, a bodybuilder, and a more slightly built man named Harry—suggested going to a graveyard that was supposedly haunted at night. Sally and Ruby took the dare. They didn't see any ghosts, but they did quickly realize the graveyard was covered with bear traps. Leonard, the body-builder, panicked and was close to hysteria because he didn't want to get hurt. Harry found a branch to brush the ground in front of him and told the women to get behind and follow in his footsteps. Leonard took the last spot in line.

This experience changed Ruby's tune. She realized that the man she wanted didn't have to be strong enough to carry her. Plus, how many burning buildings was she likely to encounter, anyway? The man she wanted would care enough about getting her to safety if she needed it, and be smart enough and brave enough to get the job done. A massive male body type was no longer important to her. It was responsibility level and ability to care that she was shopping for—go-to guys, she said, come in all sizes.

Love Notes
Stop practicing your bad habits.

Describe the Relationship

Typically, people have all sorts of different relationships, but for some, there's a distinct pattern of relating that they fall into over and over again—arguing a lot, for example. If the same dysfunctional pattern keeps repeating itself, then it seems likely that you were an active participant and perhaps at least partially responsible for the situation. If this is the case for you, consider taking a dating break and use the time to search for the deeper feelings behind all of the arguing. If you don't halt the problems on your end, no matter how perfect your next date may be, it's a good bet you'll end up self-sabotaging.

Maybe there were some things in past relationships that really did work for you. Maybe when you look back on certain people, you have a rosy glow and kind of miss the feeling from that particular relationship. That's good, but don't get too melancholy or immediately start looking up old lovers. There's usually a reason a relationship didn't work, and the truth is that when you do the work required to find the person that's a good match for you, the new reality is so much better than the old ever was.

> ## Love Notes
> If your past relationship had been the right one, it probably would have worked out and you wouldn't be reading this book.

LOVE STORIES: GERI

Geri was professionally successful, but she was a self-proclaimed failure at relationships. She dated bad boys and it always ended badly. The men she dated came into the relationship doing everything for her and seemed dedicated to meeting her needs (and creating some needs she didn't have before they arrived on the scene) . . . but then they'd turn on her.

Geri's last boyfriend, Marshall, citing all he had done for her (half of which Geri didn't want or need in the first place), became demanding and derisive when she refused to comply with his requests and demands. After nine months of watching Marshall use every opportunity to embarrass her in front of her friends, and being alternatively mean and then smothering, Geri told him she'd had enough. Marshall was infuriated and called her every name in the book. He was furious that she was leaving him without his agreement.

After her relationship ended, Geri decided to take a break from dating until she could raise her level of self-worth and expect better for herself from men. She needed to stop thinking that it was better to be with someone (even someone as bad as Marshall) than it was to be alone. Eventually Geri realized that being single is much better than being in an unhealthy relationship and started to look for someone who was worth her time.

Who Ended It?

This is usually a mixed bag. Even if you ended most of the relationships on your list, there will often be at least one where someone dumped you. Or, if you were left most of the time, there's probably at least one relationship that you ended up leaving. It's unusual to find a relationship where only one person is unhappy and things end "out of the blue." But even if somebody appears to have left without a hint of his intentions, that's unlikely to be true. When your man is dissatisfied, you almost always know—even if you're not fully admitting it to yourself. You may find that he is less attentive, less complimentary, less available, and definitely less loving and lovable. If you feel like he's pulling away, he very well may be. The question is for how long. All men can go into caves and be distracted by problems, outside pressures, not feeling well, or a personal obsession not connected with you. But if this is a sign of dissatisfaction, he still won't be all that attentive when it's over and will have a new reason (excuse) for why he is less loving.

If you did the ending in the majority of your relationships, perhaps you're choosing mates who are "right now"—men without much possibility for a future. Perhaps you knew you could never rely on these lovers, so even if they left you, you don't miss them that much; your heart just wasn't engaged and there wasn't much logic in your choice. You might be miserable for a while about being alone again but that may come from not having someone, not just missing the man you broke up with. Or maybe you're choosing men who are not your peers, men who would never leave because they think they're getting a better deal—because they are! But maybe you're not so sure that you're getting a good deal because you aren't. So these men choose to stay even if you don't have any intention of taking things any further because they believe that they couldn't possibly do better and you stay so you don't have to worry about being abandoned.

If the guy ended things the majority of the time, then you may need to open your eyes. You're likely choosing people who either aren't sufficiently interested in you or aren't sufficiently interested in a long-term relationship. There are plenty of men who would say they live to love. They love loving a woman and, for them, marriage is an accomplishment and, when they are in the midst of their search, sometimes even their Holy Grail. But some men will never fully commit even if they marry. If you are consistently choosing this latter group, it's time for a wake up call: you're the one who is fearful of commitment. You are picking the men who are best suited to helping you stay single.

Did They Remind You of Mom or Dad?

How many of your past lovers resembled one of your parents? Now, if either your mother or father have a spectacular personality—one you would really like to see in the man you marry—then someone who reminds you of one of your parents may be an appropriate choice. More often, however, it's likely that this guy won't be your perfect fit. It's easy to confuse love and familiarity. And familiar may be exactly what you need to avoid in your relationship future.

This confusion is easier to recognize when we take a look at some extreme cases. If someone was physically abused, neglected, or emotionally abused by a parent, they may be drawn to the personality of the abusing parent with a strong urge to prove themselves. They go find another cruel, negative person to try to win over. However, there is no such thing as a happy ending here; not only does this not solve the real problem—an insufficient sense of self-worth that keeps you from confronting your past and clearing your present of abusers—but the new severely critical mate will never be pleased. If you frustrate them by getting one thing right, they'll just find something new to criticize. Again, cases where abuse or neglect are involved are extreme, but you could still be hurting your chances of finding your soul mate by searching for one of your parents instead.

Love Notes
Not usually, but sometimes, the only mistake you've made in a relationship was the person you chose.

Putting together your Love Résumé might have stirred up old feelings of love, reminded you of a painful breakup, or brought on a flashback to an incident you'd rather have forgotten. Give yourself permission to honestly reflect, take action if needed, and focus on healing.

LOVE STORIES: PARK

Park was the firstborn to a pair of raging narcissists. She learned, as do all children of narcissists, that she was born to serve and was obliged to make her parents look good. She learned her lessons well, was an excellent student, was exceptionally polite, and was terrified of displeasing. After leaving home, she (not surprisingly) continued her role by being the perfect accessory on a man's arm and by doing whatever was expected—all at the expense of her own happiness and personal development. Her choices of financially successful, good-looking men were a great sense of pleasure to her parents; whether or not they were emotionally suited for their daughter was of little consequence. Park fortunately did not marry any of these men but felt incapable of breaking the mode. Therapy offered her the insight but she was not able to make the next essential step: change.

Her big break came from outside. Her boss and mentor was suddenly jettisoned into a high-profile international position and accepted with the provision that Park take his place at the company because she was the only one who could step into his shoes without additional training or down time.

> ## Love Notes
> *You know you're on the track of mature love when you're not trying to replicate a parent or choose the extreme opposite of a parent. Your goal is to choose someone who fits you now and for the future.*

Her success did not settle well with Maxim, her boyfriend at the time, who was only concerned that she could no longer pick up his dry cleaning or go where he wanted when he wanted. Park's parents enjoyed the glory of her promotion but sympathized with Maxim. They unrealistically expected her to do well at work, fulfill her boyfriend's every wish, and visit them just as often. Park failed to comply with the latter two and, in the midst of failing in her personal relationships, discovered the pleasure of succeeding at something of her own. Eventually Maxim dumped Park and her parents practically took themselves out of her life. But both events brought more relief than sorrow.

Park took a dating sabbatical. When she began again she was shopping for someone who had as much to offer her as she offered him. She wanted a helpmate instead of a tyrant and a partner instead of a man convinced of his superiority. She learned to take as well as give and decided to not introduce a man to or talk about her selections to her parents until she had decided that she had found a keeper. By the time she did, she was as devoted and committed to him as she was to her job, and her usually opinionated parents were left nearly speechless by her happiness with her dream mate.

What Did You Learn?

The purpose of the Love Résumé is to see for yourself what you have chosen and then to make decisions about what you want to change. Your heart may have been involved in many of these situations, but now it's time to put your brain to work and take a look at what your Love Résumé can teach you.

The earlier relationships outlined on many Love Résumés are often the ones that don't make any sense at all. Most of the time the men in these early relationships are ineligible for marriage, inappropriate, and look like practice material because they *were* practice material. Oftentimes women look back at their Love Résumés and realize that they are making choices that make very little sense for someone who is looking for marriage. When these women look at their past in black and white, they realize that if they don't change something to break the cadence, they'll just be adding another name to the chart without getting any closer to their goal of a committed relationship.

On healthy charts, you'll see women who have been playing around with relationships, trying to figure out exactly what and whom they want. On these charts you can almost draw a line between past mistakes, and where they figured it out and suddenly started to date "eligibles," men who could be keepers. If you have drawn that line, and the first person on the other side doesn't work out, don't panic! It's easy to feel that he is the only one like him in the whole, wide world. That's because in your experience, this person is the only "eligible" or marriage-worthy man in the whole, wide world—so far. But the truth is that there are still plenty of fish. You just haven't been fishing in the right body of water. Once you realize what you're looking for in a soul mate, it's much easier to know one when you see one.

Be Honest with Yourself

If you have a low sense of self-worth, or if you haven't given your-self the time and space to think about what you do or don't want in a mate, it's easy to get caught up in the idea of just wanting to be with someone because you and/or everyone around you thinks you should. But some women just aren't interested in putting forth the effort required for finding and keeping a man, and oftentimes, women who swear they're looking for a partner discover that they actually have a great deal of ambivalence about relationships. They talk about wanting to get married, but act as though they want to remain single. Maybe these women aren't prepared to make the life adjustments that relationships require, including self-revelation, mutuality, and making the requisite time available. Quality time can't exist without quantity time and sometimes a woman just doesn't want to give up any of the time she has to herself or doesn't want to sacrifice the time she gives to her family, children, friends, or work. If this sounds like you, you have to make some choices. Making a half-hearted attempt when you're not ready won't get you very far and can be depressing. If marriage is a real goal for you, then you need to get serious and start acting like someone who can commit to a long-term relationship. If you feel that now is not the right time for you, or if you really have too much going on, don't feel pressured to find a man right now; true love will still be out there when you really are ready to let it in.

Some women also struggle with overcompensation. Perhaps you act overly independent and secure in the way your life is now as a way to let your dates know that you're not needy or codependent. While being happy with your life and projecting a positive outlook is better than acting dejected, lonely, and in need of adoption, don't overdo it. If you send the message that you're completely happy being alone, why would anyone put forth the time and effort to try to make you part of a couple?

LOVE STORIES: CAROLE

Carole was a very forceful CEO of a large company. She received tremendous acclaim from her boss and peers. In fact, she thought she was practically perfect, and therefore needed the perfect mate to suit her. She was married to her job, but wanted an appropriate husband who would be supportive of having their life revolve around her work and help her look good to her company and clients. Carole was trying to fill a slot, not fall in love.

The man Carole was looking for could only fit into her picture; she had no intention of fitting into his. Not surprisingly, her selfishness was not getting her far. Nobody wants to feel like a commodity, and everyone takes love personally. It was only when Carole was honest with herself about wanting companionship and love, and only when she admitted that she did often feel lonely, that she was able to move forward with intent. She needed to redefine what "dream mate" meant to her, accept her own vulnerability, and let it show. Carole remained a dynamo at work, but when it came to love, she became more interested in feeling good than looking good. She eventually developed a softness that ultimately attracted men who connected with her personally and were not only willing, but proud to escort her to official office functions as well.

BE HONEST WITH YOURSELF QUIZ, PART 1:
Are You Still Acting Single?

You may say you want to get married, but you could actually be coming across as someone who wants to stay unattached at all costs. To find out if you're still acting single, answer yes or no to each of the following questions.

1. Do you feel already married to your job, children, or parents?
2. Do you make potential dates jump hurdles to get a piece of your time?
3. Are you dismissive, combative, or wary in the way you relate to a man?
4. Do you put little effort in your appearance because you say you want to be sure people are attracted to the "real you"?
5. Did your recovery from a bad relationship take more time than the actual relationship itself?
6. Are you dissatisfied and always trying to change other people?

If you answered yes to two or more questions, you are blocking relationships and need to act more eligible, available, and interested, rather than indifferent and emotionally distant.

BE HONEST WITH YOURSELF QUIZ, PART 2:
Do You Really Want to Get Married?

To discover if you're really ready to tie the knot, answer yes or no to each of the following questions.

1. Are you prepared to take the time to meet, date, and court?
2. Do you want to move career, family, friends, pets, or unsuitable lovers from the top-priority positions in your life?
3. Would you enjoy self-revelation with your spouse?
4. Do you get more gratification out of the long run in a relationship than the startup period?
5. Do you wish to give up some of your privacy and alone time?
6. Do you want to be available to the other person?
7. Are you able to be both independent and dependent?
8. When in love, can you state your own point of view?
9. Are you able to think in terms of mutual interest on a daily basis?

If you answered no to three or more questions, you have emotional blocks to being married. Do you want to change? Then use these questions as goals for your behavioral changes. Refer back to these goals daily until your new habits are set.

Take the time you need to reflect on what you've learned. When you've cleared out the emotional cobwebs of your past, you're ready for the work required to find, seduce, know, and keep your dream mate. But before you get to that point, it's important to figure out what you're really looking for in a man.

Chapter 2

Figure Out What You
Want in a Mate

Myth: You're only compatible with your type.
Truth: Any good person could be your type.

Once you've come to terms with your dating history, you can start the fun part: imagining your future. But just as you wouldn't go to the store without some idea of what you want to buy (lest you end up with a cart full of something that's not good for you), you shouldn't begin dating without a clear idea of what you're looking for in your ideal mate.

It's time to figure out exactly what you're looking for by putting together a Spouse Shopping List. Instead of listing milk, bread, and cookie-dough ice cream, here you will specify everything you want and need in a mate. No one will grade it. Preferably no one else will ever see it, because it's not about pleasing anyone other than you. Have fun!

Fill Out Your Spouse Shopping List

To fill out your Spouse Shopping List, follow the instructions below. I've included a blank list later on so you can get right to it!

Column 1: Write down everything you want in a man. Don't edit yourself. Don't think. Don't evaluate. If it comes to mind, write it down. After you've included the basics of what you want, push onward. Is there any private little dream or fantasy you have? Consider everything that you want and put it all down on paper so you'll be able to keep it in mind for the future.

Column 2: What is unacceptable to you? List everything you really couldn't stand in a mate. Don't try to be nice or kind—just honest.

Column 3: Finally, negotiate with yourself. Decide if you're flexible on anything in the "Requirements" column.

> ## Love Notes
> *Don't go shopping for food or love without knowing what you want and need.*

Sample Spouse Shopping List

In case you weren't sure about any of the categories, here are some examples to get you thinking.

Shopping List Category	Requirements	Unacceptable	Negotiable
Chemistry/ Attraction	Great sex, terrific smile, fit body	Ugly	Medium body
Spiritual or Religious Values	Non-judgmental Christian; semi-regular church attendance	Agnostic or atheist	Spiritual person
Status/Money	Financial comfort and responsibility	Debts, laziness, lack of responsibility	N/A
Appearance	Clean, neat, attractive, well-dressed	Poor hygiene	Poor taste in clothes—as long as I can give fashion advice in the future
Communication Style	Very verbal; non-combative	Poor grammar, verbally abusive	Usually holds in his feelings, but will open up to me when it comes to important matters

Shopping List Category	Requirements	Unacceptable	Negotiable
Taste Level/Style	Shares mine in people and home furnishings	Loud '70s music	Music of any kind if non-continuous
Social Level/Frequency	Social butterfly, more out than in, never met a stranger, my family likes him	Invites people to house without warning, talks more to the waiter than me	Doesn't have to go out every time I do
Activity Level/Type	Plays tennis and golf regularly	Couch or mouse potato	He won't complain if I play tennis and golf with my friends
Leadership in Relationship	Partnership	Domineering	N/A
Other	Best friend	N/A	N/A

Spouse Shopping List

Here's a blank shopping list for you to fill in. Write down everything that comes to mind in every category.

Shopping List Category	Requirements	Unacceptable	Negotiable
Chemistry/Attraction			
Spiritual or Religious Values			
Status/Money			
Appearance			
Communication Style			
Taste Level/Style			
Social Level/Frequency			
Activity Level/Type			
Leadership in Relationship			
Other			

Analyze Your List

You may know what you would choose, but you also need to know why. Closer introspection can help you understand yourself and could convince you to re-evaluate what may have once been a very strong preference or an old fear, and may help you move some of your "requirements" and "unacceptables" to the "negotiable" column.

> ### Love Notes
> *Both partners need to believe they're getting a great deal.*

Chemistry/Attraction

You don't really have to kiss a lot of frogs; they're slimy. But you do need to define your prince with some latitude. Some women want to feel that high when their man walks in the room. Others need a soulful connection and a sense of being meant for each other. Still others are most attracted to a sense of ease, comfort, and security. Whatever turns the lights on for you is fine. You need to do what you need to do. Have what you want. But keep in mind that at the end of the day, you kiss a person, not a face.

Spiritual or Religious Values

Religion is important, especially if you have—or want—children. Think about what you truly want in this area. Some women want to be with someone who believes exactly what they believe, but others don't need a co-participant. Depending on your own personal views, you may be able to accept someone without perfect church attendance as long as you believe that your faith or your spirituality is compatible. And if you're not religious, you may be able to accept someone who is religious or spiritual, as long as that person is nonjudgmental or evangelical. Usually, it's the concepts of faith and belief that need to match—along with acceptance and support—rather than day-in day-out religious practice.

For those who must have somebody with beliefs and habits identical to theirs, a word of caution: just as meeting a great person in a bar can mean you later discover the only thing you have in common is drinking, somebody in your own church, synagogue, temple, or mosque may feel perfect at first, but you will need to have much more in common than just religion. If it is your religious match that you need, don't settle. Get what you want, just realize that finding a man who has one thing that you want doesn't make him perfect for you in other areas. But as you search, keep in mind that there's no right or wrong about finding your dream mate; you need to look for those things that matter to you. The important thing is to be very clear about what you expect of a mate.

Status/Money

Status and money matter, but the major question is: matters to whom? The showoff partner at reunions and parties is great, but it is your daily living with your spouse that is of prime importance. Do not settle for less if you want a sophisticated, powerful, highly educated member of an upper socioeconomic group. But keep well in mind that what matters most is how you feel about yourself when you are with him; you're looking for a man, not a stereotype.

> **Love Notes**
> No one is rich or famous enough to be worth feeling worse about yourself.

Appearance

Appearance is a broader concept than it first appears. When we're talking about appearance, we're not just referring to a great build, gorgeous hair, or sparkling eyes, but also hygiene, manner of dress, and overall presentation, which have more to do with attractiveness and draw than an individual feature. Most women aren't looking for someone "gorgeous," but they do want someone who is presentable and smells good, rather than someone who is sloppy, slouchy, and less than squeaky clean. They want a mate who can go anywhere, who doesn't have really terrible teeth and bad breath, etc. But keep in mind that appearance and attractiveness can vary according to age or taste. For example, a slightly sloppy or casual dresser may be viewed as an appealing individualist to a twenties to forties crowd. But for the fifties and growing, these qualities are more likely to be viewed as anti-society or as the traits of a chronic underachiever.

> **Love Notes**
> *The ugly truth is that appearances matter.*

That said, please remember that some things are imminently fixable and changeable. Many women can't get past a bad haircut, clothes that went out decades ago, or faces hidden behind a beard and oversized glasses, but relying too much on these traits can cause you to make your dating pool a little too shallow. Just keep in mind that appearances can change, and most men are willing to heed the fashion advice of their significant other—particularly if you are willing to do the shopping.

LOVE STORIES: STEVE

Steve, a thirty-seven-year-old children's book author, looked like central casting's idea of a bad date. He was a very thin six foot four and wasn't the best dresser. A typical outfit for Steve was likely to include a rumpled shirt, garish tie, old jeans, and a Windbreaker, items that worked together to give even the kindest woman pause. Steve took my class courtesy of his mother, who also gave him a care package that contained enrollment in a dating service and a gift certificate for a nice department store (specifying that it was only good in the men's department, not the electronics section). On top of the gift box in large letters, his mother had written, "I WANT GRANDCHILDREN!" Subtle woman, but she got him there.

> ## Love Notes
> *Most men will dress differently if they get a positive physical reaction. In short: they usually don't care that much about clothes, but they do care about getting laid.*

By the end of the course, Steve had transformed both his look and the way he presented himself. He had committed to being truly open to meeting new women and now looked like someone a girl would want to date instead of someone who was totally clueless about what women found attractive. He was an eligible guy and now he looked like one.

After class, quite a few women gathered around Steve to talk. One woman cut through the gaggle and asked him to go have a cup of coffee with her on the spot. Now they're married.

Communication Style

The communication styles of you and your prospective spouse must match at some level. Some happy couples fight; some don't. Some talk a lot, and some don't talk much at all. It doesn't matter so much how you communicate, as long as you connect with your partner. Communication is an ongoing lesson requiring effort and feedback. Some important communication "lessons" include:

1. **How to listen:** If you weren't really listened to as a child, or if all your parents did was listen to you, you might not be a great

listener. But, as we will cover many times throughout the book, in order for someone to feel loved, he needs to feel understood. And in order for you to understand someone, you must learn to listen to him—both his words and his actions.

2. **"Sandwiching" your needs requests with positive regard and affection before and after:** Telling a man you need more from him can make him feel inadequate, and may be less likely to get you what you want. But if you communicate how much you love him, how wonderful what he already gives is, and how your request will only enhance what the two of you have, you're much more likely to get what you need—and you'll spare his feelings while you're at it.

3. **Building self-esteem in yourself and your mate:** You can marry someone who is worlds away from you—one of you could be a high-level banker and the other a line worker—but your self-esteem levels are likely to be similar and need to be maintained. The more you and your partner believe you deserve the best and have the best, the better you will be to each other and the stronger your relationship will be for years to come.

Remember: No one is a mind reader so make the time to share your needs and to listen to the needs of your partner. Always do it with love and respect.

> **Love Notes**
> *Still waters don't necessarily run deep.*

Taste Level/Style

Taste and style are, of course, in the eye of the beholder. One person's gasp of horror would be another person's "Wow!" This may be one of the areas where you need to determine who's the boss. Compromise is usually treated as king in relationships, but it has its limits. If styles are divergent, they cannot just be shuffled together to achieve a look that either mate wants. However, if there is enough space, divergent opinions can mean one person has a room to their own liking, with the more house-proud person leaving that particular door shut when company is over. In this case, it may be necessary to have one person be completely pleased and the other genuinely happy to concede.

Social Level/Frequency

Extroverts and introverts do tend to attract each other. For these people, compromises do need to be struck. A high-energy socializer could end up terrorizing a more introverted spouse while following the lead of the true introvert could take all the life out of the extrovert. The good thing is that deals can be struck in any direction. Usually a good introvert/extrovert relationship works with the extrovert wanting—and making time for—more contact with people and the introvert being willing to join them at regular intervals. Make sure you're very open about your needs way ahead of vows in order not to engender resentment down the road.

Activity Level

This can be a tricky category in which to compromise. Many active people wouldn't do well with a couch potato and someone who thinks the out-of-doors is something to view through a window would be a nervous wreck around a high-energy person pushing them to participate. However, if you're a former couch potato who has just started walking and aspires to run, you might like to date a seasoned runner who will coach, inspire, and motivate you. Or maybe you're a former athlete who has had a serious injury and would appreciate a man content to watch movies on the couch and take care of you. But no matter where you fall on the spectrum, be honest about it up front.

Leadership

Nothing is ever precisely 50/50 and that goes for relationships as well. When you're involved with someone, one of you will take on the leadership role, even though categories can change and each of you may be the leader in your own areas of skill. Just be sure that you and your partner are in agreement about who plays which role, at which points, in your relationship.

> **Love Notes**
> *Don't expect a whole lot more than you're willing to offer.*

Other

Chances are that your list has at least one relatively unimportant detail about which you're being too much of a stickler. Almost everybody comes up with at least one thing they can live without and many women fall in love with someone quite different than they expected. Take this opportunity to go back to your negotiable column and, if applicable, fill in some blanks with a more open-minded perspective. Assume you've gotten everything else you wanted, then, line-by-line, negotiate with yourself to try to plump up this column.

How Your List Can Help or Hurt You

Now that you've created and analyzed your list, it's time for you to realize that your expectations can both help and hurt you when it comes to finding true love. This is especially true if you found that your list was especially long. While a long list can help you figure out exactly what you're looking for, in some cases, long lists contain contradictory desires that can set you up for relationship failure right off the bat. For example, if your list has you looking for an adoring snuggler who only wants to be with you, but you also want a man's man who spends a lot of time with his buddies chances are you're going to have to compromise somewhere. No man out there will have everything that you're looking for, and the more you want, the harder it will be to find someone who fits all of your specifications.

LOVE STORIES: MAI LIN

Mai Lin's friends dubbed her "hard to please." She had a long list of criteria that a man needed to meet for her to feel she wasn't wasting her time by accepting a date. Income was a priority. A potential mate had to make what she made or more. He needed to be at least her height when she was wearing her tallest heels. She preferred a man with at least a master's degree. Physically, he had to have straight teeth and be a sharp dresser. He had to be confident, maybe even slightly arrogant, and he had to be good with children.

After taking a good look at her Spouse Shopping List, Mai Lin's priorities began to change. She realized that these more superficial attributes weren't as important as traits like lovingness, honesty, and compatibility. Instead of requiring a snazzy dresser, she became willing to consider men who were neat and well-groomed. She also became open to men who were confident, not arrogant, realizing arrogance can be a cover up for low self-esteem. Straight teeth were no longer a requirement (after all, hers weren't model-perfect), and a master's degree wasn't a necessity, although she still preferred a man with a career not a job. Her dream mate still needed to be great with kids, since Mai Lin was a single mom.

"There is no point in making a long list of criteria that no one on the planet can meet," Mai Lin e-mailed me after class. "I felt I was missing out on a lot of good guys because I was convinced that there was a type of man I was looking for. All that matters is that we get along, can be or become financially stable together, and can accept each other for who we both are."

Go back and look at your list. Are you as hard to please as Mai Lin was? Is your list of requirements long enough to qualify as a love block? If so, it's probably time for a reality check. Ask yourself what you can live with. What do you consider to be deal breakers? Having a good idea of where you're willing to compromise will serve you well as you search for your soul mate.

> ## Love Notes
> *Get smart: You're looking for compatible intelligence, not the so-called proof of it.*

Make Your List Work for You

But having a long list isn't always a bad thing. Some people have really long lists and manage to get what they want by sacrificing in a category that may mean a lot to others but not them.

LOVE STORIES: LINDSEY

Lindsey had eighteen line items on her Spouse Shopping List. She ended up marrying someone with three extremely difficult children who lived with them. She had to move to a different city that she didn't like, quit her job, and leave her friends and family. But stepchildren and life swapping weren't a big problem for Lindsey, and she was able to find all eighteen of the traits she was looking for in one man.

In addition, if you have a long list, but all of the items are attainable and none are contradictory for the personality type you're seeking, it can work. Most of the time having a long list doesn't work out, but you may be one of the lucky ones. Take a look at your list and find out.

LOVE STORIES: HILLARY

Set up by mutual friends, Hillary and Marc were pleasantly surprised when they first met each other for coffee. Marc couldn't believe such a beautiful lady was available. But halfway through the first latte, Hillary made her dating requirements very clear. She expected flowers at least twice a week, phone calls twice a day, and on weekends she expected to spend Friday through Sunday at his place.

These were all things on her mental Shopping List but by voicing them to each prospective partner, they became a protective shield against marriage. Hillary voiced wanting to marry but was scared to death. By being sufficiently obnoxious, she narrowed her chances of getting a second date which, quasiconsciously was exactly the point.

But there was a happy ending. By degrees, Hillary dropped her armor. She became less guarded and learned how to stop being so bossy. She quelled her commitment anxieties well enough to wait to find out what her date wanted to give and when. Her reward was she knew her date's actions were genuine, which provided her with a far greater sense of security than her illusion of control could ever bring.

As you search for your dream mate, remember that you're looking for a partner here on earth, not a god or a superhero. Shop in your own galaxy, trim down your long list, and get ready to find a committed man.

Hide Your List

Now that you've filled out your edited Spouse Shopping List, hide it for a while. Seriously! It's a written goal sheet and safety net—not a job application that you take along on your dates. No matter what you do, don't confuse a first date with an interview. Your date will know if you are mentally checking off boxes, and feeling like a job applicant is not sexy; first dates are awkward enough without a quiz portion. And keep in mind that you won't find out everything about your date the first time you go out together. He may be wary of speaking about his spirituality the first time you meet, but you might find after he warms up to you on date two or three that he's just as religious as you. He may not want to reveal his obsession with Netflix on a first date, but you could discover your mutual love of classic movies on the third.

While you're learning about him, do your best to be yourself; don't just go out there and play the role of a "great date." Instead, be confident in who you are and realize that sometimes who you are is more than good enough.

LOVE STORIES: APRIL

April had fifteen requirements on her shopping list. It was clear she attended every first date, list in mind like a weapon, with more than a slight leaning toward ruling each guy out. And she did, time after time after time. The men knew this because she gave the impression she was interviewing, checking off each requirement as it was fulfilled or not fulfilled. No one likes to feel like a stack of requirements. One date actually asked, "Did I pass?" Needless to say, he—like everyone else—did not.

One of my clients told me that you don't make business deals on the golf course, but you do assess character. This is a good analogy that can be applied to dating. When you golf, golf. When you date, date! Wait at least three to five dates before bringing the checklist back out (when you're alone!) to assess whether or not this man meets your expectations. When the list re-emerges, you may find that this man you're very compatible with doesn't meet all thirteen of your requirements, but that the three most important ones are all there. And if you meet someone who makes you feel wonderful, adores you, and is eligible and marriage-worthy, you might decide to throw your list out the window. And that's okay, too.

Remember, the challenge is to always take your best behavior with you on a date and into marriage. Whether or not you have a successful relationship is completely up to you. In the next chapter, you'll learn how to stop being your own worst enemy—and how to let love in.

Chapter 3

Stop Being Your Own Worst Enemy

Myth: There are no good single men out there.
Truth: There are plenty of good single men out there, you just have to get out of your own way and go out of your way to find one.

If you're ever ended a relationship by saying, "It's not you, it's me," you may not mean it. You might even be thinking, "You have such a terrifying temper, a rabid dog would be more inviting," or "You're so controlling I can't even take a shower without you pacing outside the door." But no matter how objectionable *he* may be, *you* are still the problem. You can make all of the excuses you want for why you're not already living happily with your dream partner, and blame your failed relationships on past lovers. But when it comes down to it, you're single because of you, not because there aren't enough marriage-worthy people out there, or because no one is good enough, or even because everyone you date always turns out to be crazy. Perhaps your expectations are too high, or maybe you choose people you know will help create a train wreck because you're afraid of commitment.

We all have an amazing capacity for creative avoidance, and most of us cherish our favorite delusions. I've seen some impossible to please *amoro-phobics*, people pathologically fearful of love, dig some really deep holes for themselves using everything from an obnoxious demeanor to homeless-person couture. These women may doubt their ability to find, create, and maintain loving relationships, but they may not even recognize that they've been getting in their own way! But it doesn't have to be like this for you. Here you'll learn both what to avoid when you're looking for love and how to say good-bye to your past—for good!

Top Love Blocks to Avoid

Love blocks are the stumbling blocks we consciously or quasi-consciously put in our paths that prevent success in love or at least slow down the process—sometimes to glacial speed. By tripping ourselves along the road, momentum is lost and rewards harder to gain. But unlike roadblocks, the love blocks we create are often far less visible. They're built out of anger, resentment, and negativity, but most often they're built out of fear. Love blocks can stop a happy relationship dead in its tracks or paralyze one half of a loving couple. The point is that you should avoid putting these blocks up at all, and even if you've already erected a few on your path, there are things you can and should do to tear them down. By tripping yourself up along the road, momentum is lost and the reward (a healthy relationship) is harder to gain. To be sure you are in prime shape for the road ahead, it's important to identify the most common love blocks and do whatever you can to discover them right away.

Wasting Time

The Scarlett O'Hara "tomorrow is another day" school of time management is particularly prominent in the area of love. Tomorrow may be another day, but why waste today with someone who is not right for you? Some people waste months, years, even decades, with the wrong person, and had they been honest with themselves, they probably would have seen the signs from the very beginning.

LOVE STORIES: MELISSA

Melissa, a single mother with a five-year-old daughter, had been with her boyfriend, Hunter, for four years. She came to see me because she felt like she couldn't get him to commit and she was ready to get married. After just one session, it was very clear that

Melissa was no longer in love with Hunter, and had fallen out of love with him at least a year before. Not so coincidentally, it was around the time he started using drugs and stopped showing her any affection. I asked Melissa why on earth she wanted this marriage instead of finding someone drug-free and loving. Her answer was "I've put four years into this relationship. Do you know how hard it is to find a man who is okay dating a woman with a child? I can't do all of this over again."

Melissa felt like she had already wasted so much time with her boyfriend that it was easier to marry him (and perhaps commit to a life of misery) than start over. But every day she stayed in the relationship was another day she could have spent searching for a good partner for herself and a father figure for her daughter. After some work, Melissa began to realize that marrying an addict with no wish to change guaranteed a downhill ride, and that anybody who made her feel less good about herself as a woman would be disastrous for her and her child. She did leave Hunter and found her equilibrium as a family of two. She's not dating anyone seriously as of right now, but she's happier and more secure than she ever was when she was with Hunter—and her daughter is, too.

> ### Love Notes
> *If you are unhappy and dissatisfied, wasting time is a really good method for staying that way.*

It's easy for people to feel like they have all the time in the world when it comes to dating. And while no one actually runs out of time to fall in love and get married, a single woman can become circumstantially depressed when she feels she is out of time. So, please don't even have another cup of coffee with someone you know deep-down is wrong for you.

QUIZ: Are You a Time Waster?

Are you wasting valuable time and energy on the wrong people when you could be using that time to meet your dream mate? To find out if you're a time waster answer yes or no to each of the following questions.

1. Have you stayed in a relationship just because you wanted to avoid the breakup?
2. Have you dated people you knew were wrong for you because "It's better to date someone than no one at all"?
3. Have you ever rekindled a flame with an ex-lover out of boredom or desperation?
4. Do you spend more time thinking about your past relationships than what you want out of a future relationship?
5. Have you ever said yes to a date you did not want because you didn't want to hurt the guy's feelings?
6. Have you ever said yes to a second or third date because you were too uncomfortable to say no?

If you answered yes to two or more questions, you are wasting time. Forget Mr. Right Now and put your valuable time and effort into finding Mr. Right.

Hoping

You wouldn't just hope that someone would get a job for you, or take care of your health; if you did, you'd starve or die. Instead, you'd apply for jobs and schedule interviews, or call a doctor and follow directions to get well again. Hoping that a potential date will take all of the initiative and ask you out—or be really nice and just descend from your living room ceiling—is another way of stalling romance and starving your love life.

If you're interested in a man, make sure that he knows you're interested by being a fabulous flirt: Smile copiously, tell him how wonderful it is to be with him, slowly stroll by his table (more than once if you need to), approach him and start a conversation, or extend a foot in his path to get him to drop at your feet (trip him if you need to). Just make sure the guy you have your eyes on gets the message.

Don't let the action stop there either. Be assertive and make the phone call you've been sitting around waiting for. Ask your friends or family to push you out of your familiar world and cheer you on when you take risks. And temporarily divorce your dark side "support" group, who want you to bond with their fears and frustrations. You're not going to find a great guy if you're spending all your time eating ice cream and bitching with your disillusioned girlfriends about how much you hate men. A good support group helps you feel optimistic, grounded, and deserving.

LOVE STORIES: BONNIE MAE

Bonnie Mae had a "good" girlfriend, Wynn. Their pact was to support each other in their soul mate search, but Bonnie Mae began to feel she had a pact with an identity snatcher. Wynn would call multiple times daily and text frantically if her friend couldn't be reached. She insisted on knowing everything Bonnie Mae wore, where she was going, who her dates were, and where she was going to meet them. Once she had the info, Wynn would go to the same stores, buy the same outfits, and show up wherever Bonnie Mae went. When Wynn arrived on the scene, she would fawn over her friend, but between copious compliments and talking about every detail of her life, she dominated the evening.

The crash course in how to get rid of what isn't good for you came when they both went on an online dating service. Their agreement was to notify each other when either of them responded to or contacted a man so the other wouldn't be competing. Day one, Bonnie Mae e-mailed the screen names of the three men and received the forty-nine screen names of the men Wynn believed she had rendered unavailable by putting them on her list. That finally did it. Bonnie Mae knew she was feeling less than happy around her "friend," but it was this instance that made her realize Wynn was sapping her dating energy and happily taking away her dating pool—not because Wynn could use them all, but because she was hoarding for the sake of feeling that she had more. Bonnie Mae ended this friendship and felt free.

Retaining Guilt

If you feel guilty when you say no—not just to potential dates, but to anyone—your time is getting eaten up. You have the right to make your own decisions and live your life as you choose. When you say yes to things you don't want to do or don't have time to do, you basically tell yourself that the person who asked is more important than you. Have you ever said yes to something, and then felt resentful about it later? Then you need to slow your rate of acceptance. Learn this phrase: "I'm not sure, I'll have to double-check my schedule." It gives you time to think, and your schedule could say you have a commitment to spend time on yourself. If you don't make it clear that your time is valuable, how can you expect anyone else to know it?

LOVE STORIES: MARLA

For years Marla had joined her married siblings for dinner at their parents' house every Saturday night, but when she started to take her goal of getting married seriously, she realized that she needed Saturday nights for meeting new people and dating. Telling her family she'd wouldn't be joining them for dinner on Saturdays was like starting World War III. Marla explained her reasons and offered to get together another night of the week, but they were not listening. The brouhaha that ensued made one thing clear: Marla's family's agenda for her romantic future (or lack thereof) did not match her goals. But Marla stood firm. She did say no to her family's schedule but made time to see everyone at times that were mutually agreeable.

Decide to do fewer favors for friends, stop listening to anyone who repeatedly complains about the same unfixed problem, and cut back on overtime at work or an overload of volunteer work. You will need to retrieve some of the hours you now spend elsewhere for not only having dates, but being able to relax and take the time to set the right attitude for them. Your goal is to find and keep your dream mate, not to remain tired, grumpy, and single.

> ## Love Notes
> *Harried is not anyone's best date look.*

If you're truly ready to kick guilt to the curb, there are three simple steps that you must undertake:

1. Turn your "yes" into "I'll think about that and let you know."
2. Do think about what you will sacrifice to put this item on your to-do list. After you've had some time to think, you may realize you don't have the time, or don't want to do what's being asked of you. And that's okay!
3. Just say no. Then spend that time working on yourself and finding your dream mate.

So forget about guilt. After all, allowing yourself the time and space to make your own decisions will raise your happiness level and allow you to have the emotional room to give your new mate the time and attention he deserves.

Keeping Old Baggage and Emotional Clutter

To be in the best condition possible for this twelve-month plan, you need to eliminate toxic people from your life. You may have friends and family who are energy vampires (people who seem to suck the life right out of you—blamers, controllers, time gobblers). Or there may be someone who can ruin your mood with even the briefest of contact.

While it's impossible to eliminate everyone (like your boss, for instance) who may be destructive, this is the year to consider either breaking the chain to these toxic people, or taking a sabbatical to give you your best possible shot at reaching your goal. As for your dates or relationships, here is whom you need to leave behind:

> **Love Notes**
> *If you feel worse about yourself when you're around someone, he isn't worth being around.*

- Anyone who wants to have a phone or e-mail relationship instead of wanting to be with you in person
- Anyone who is married, in love with themselves, or emotionally or physically unavailable
- Anyone abusive
- Anyone who doesn't help you feel good about yourself
- Anyone you don't think you can please
- Anyone unable to express or hear feelings
- Anyone dishonest
- Anyone with sex, alcohol, gambling, shopping, or drug addictions
- Anyone disrespectful of you or your background
- Anyone who doesn't love you back
- Anyone who has not gotten more comfortable with intimacy and closer to you in the time you've been together

Need some help? Write down or record every bad thing you have to say about each of the romances you need to leave. If it's on paper, put it in an envelope, and if it's recorded, burn it to CD. Put a bow (black or pink—your choice) on it and hide it. If you ever get into that time-wasting lull of musing over that person, open your reminder of the reality.

Lack of Self-Awareness

It's often easier to see the faults in others instead of recognizing your own. In fact, sometimes the things you dislike the most about other people are the things you might not like about yourself. Perhaps it's time for a wakeup call: If there's always something wrong with them, then there's definitely something wrong with you. If you keep dating commitment-phobics, then you are one. If you stay with sexist men, then you believe you deserve their slurs and derision. Work on building your self-esteem (which we'll do a lot more of in the next chapter), and these ineligible lovers will go out and find other victims. Best of all, as a confident and comfortable person, you are more attractive as a friend, date, and mate.

> **Love Notes**
> *Heed the old cliché: when you point a finger, there are three more pointing back at you.*

Self-Indulgence

Nothing dampens a love relationship faster than yelling, meanness, and overall immaturity. After all, it takes a grownup to have a good marriage; in fact, it takes two. Character assassination is not foreplay. Keep in mind that unfiltered communications do not create connection. They only create space between two people who love each other. Be sure you are telling your partner how you feel gently and concisely, don't tell some mangled version that will make him feel bad and puzzled and you frustrated. Considering your partner in thought, word, and deed is infinitely preferable to saying and doing what you want when you want with low-level consideration and kindness. Not sure about your maturity level? Take the following quiz to see how grown up you really are.

MATURITY-LEVEL Assessment Quiz

To find out how mature you are, ask yourself if you . . .

A. Get extremely upset when disappointed?
B. Express your love and appreciation?

A. Blame, criticize, and judge?
B. Take reasonable responsibility?

A. Sulk or stop speaking for days when upset?
B. Work with your lover on conflict resolution?

A. Keep an angry/negative view of your lover?
B. Have a positive attitude most of the time?

A. Get defensive when hearing a complaint?
B. Listen and learn from suggestions?

Answering yes to two or more questions in the "A" series or no to three or more in the "B" series means that your insecurity and low self-esteem are preventing the mastering of good relationship skills. Practice the "B" series on dates. It will help you be more accepting and more likely to keep the ones you want, as well as help you with your personal growth.

Love Notes

Add this to your to-do list:
Make maturity a goal this year.

Perfectionism

If you are a perfectionist, you know it, and your friends and family have undoubtedly pointed it out to you a time or two. No one is perfect, and no one ever will be—but for whatever reason, people still cling to the illusion. At one time or another, everyone wants to be gorgeous, rich, slim, loved, famous, smart, witty, creative, etc. But you can't be everything. And the sooner you realize that, the easier life will be for you and everyone else around you. If you don't love yourself the way you are, how can you expect anyone else to? Imagine how difficult it would be to please a perfectionist partner. Accepting your own lack of perfection means realizing that the person you marry will be imperfect, as will your relationship. Be real. Focus on positive attributes— yours and theirs. Also remember: perfect is boring.

> **Love Notes**
> Perfectionism blocks you from happiness, excellence, and your own personal best. So do yourself a favor and stop being so hard on yourself and everyone else.

Negativity

Showing compassion and caring to the people around you advertises your ability to love, while hateful or critical behavior exposes self-centeredness. You simply cannot be viewed as a warm and likeable person when you keep thinking that "all men are pigs" or "all men will use me and leave me." Bad attitudes severely limit the men whom you find acceptable and then, if you do find someone, chances are you'll run him off because you're so unpleasant and negative.

Go on a negativity diet. Choose only three reasons you can use to eliminate a potential mate (e.g., smoking, poor grooming, and wandering eyes) and only rule out men based on those three reasons.

Looking for the good in people means that you are more likely to find it, and in turn, you might start to appreciate even more good in yourself. Plus, being positive is infectious. By lifting the spirits of everyone around you, you feel good and are more attractive as a date or mate.

Love Notes

Negativity is extremely unattractive and can doom you for failure.

Now, expecting someone (even yourself) to change overnight is a lot to ask. But there are little things you can do every hour of every day that will help you truly appreciate the value in other people and yourself.

Practice positivity. If you are the kind of person who sees what's wrong with the way a stranger across the street or across the room looks, try forcing yourself to first identify something positive. For example, if you usually notice a woman in too-tight clothes, try instead focusing on her beautiful eyes or hair. And smile at her. Chances are good she'll smile back and you will forget all about her wardrobe and focus on the pleasant interaction you just had.

Make a gratitude list. Write down the things, people, and experiences that make you feel good about your life. When you're feeling grumpy and critical, the list will be your way for remembering the good in your life, especially if they can be turned into action items, like going for a walk, petting your dog, or calling up your best friend just to talk.

Give at least one genuine compliment every day. Give at least one heartfelt compliment a day whether it's complimenting a stranger on her hat or a coworker on his performance. You'll be amazed at how happy it makes the recipient and yourself.

Once you begin to exude positivity, you'll be amazed at how it comes back to you tenfold.

Ignorance about Love

While romantic movies are enjoyable, and often give people hope for love, they paint a terrible picture of relationships. Many experts even claim "rom-coms" have made it nearly impossible for people (especially women) to be satisfied with realistic relationships. Romantic comedies, romance novels, and the like have certainly helped to create a generation or two of fantasy chasers.

Lovers may dream of being swept off their feet or to have their love affirmed in some grand gesture. And while love professed on a JumboTron during a baseball game or sending sixty roses is wonderful, it isn't a substitute for daily displays of caring, and it isn't necessarily proof that the relationship has a solid foundation. Sometimes the opposite is true. So stop looking for the grand gesture and start believing in behavior over words.

LOVE STORIES: RACHEL

After Rachel and Jeremy had been dating for three years, Rachel told him she wanted to get married soon. She was nearly thirty and wanted to have at least two children. Jeremy dodged the subject like the plague for two more years; he wouldn't communicate even his simplest fears or reservations.

A very frustrated Rachel decided she needed to take some time to think about what she really wanted from Jeremy and from her life, so she took a month-long road trip. Fearing he was losing her, Jeremy flew from the West Coast to the East Coast to surprise Rachel and tell her he was finally ready to marry her. But it was too late. With time to reflect, Rachel had decided she didn't want to spend the rest of her life with someone who refused to communicate with her when it came to big life decisions that affected them both. Jeremy flew back to California defeated and dejected.

Three months later, Rachel met a man who was as ready as she was for marriage and just as ready to talk about it. A year after they met, they were engaged.

People don't commit to other people to be ignored or left out of major life decisions. It's important to not just give what you think you should give or give one big thing here and there, but to learn what your significant other likes, wants, and needs on a daily basis. (Hint: don't assume that it's what you would choose.) Whether it's attention, support for his dreams and goals, physical and verbal affection, communication about the future, or gifts, everyone wants to be acknowledged in some way. So when you think about marriage and commitment, ask not what is in it for you, but what you can do to help your partner feel happier than he has ever felt before. If the relationship is working for both of you, you will feel nurtured and loved, as well as nurturing and loving.

QUIZ: Are You a Fantasy Chaser or a Real-World Lover?

Not sure your views about love are based in reality? Take this quiz to find out! Do You ...

1. Fall in love very quickly or wait to really learn about the other person?
2. Plan your future in the first three dates or focus on present-day relationship building?
3. Have a history of non-commitment or make every effort to keep the love you find?
4. Use fight-or-flight tactics or skillfully communicate both attachment and conflict?
5. Get disappointed or angry when your hopes aren't met or learn to accept and love unconditionally the person you have chosen?
6. Assign blame when you are dissatisfied or immediately go to work on problem solving?

Answering yes to two or more questions means it's time to get real. Stop comparing your relationships to those you see in romantic movies and start evaluating them based on fundamental building blocks like respect and reliability.

Beware: even one fantasy-chasing behavior can ruin your chances of lifelong love. Make your marriage choice based on heart, soul, and emotional intelligence.

Inability to Listen and Learn

Think back to a time when you tried to tell a story or communicate a message to someone who was staring at the TV or computer, texting, or playing a game. Perhaps your boss only listens to half of your ideas. Maybe you had a parent who read the newspaper while you tried to tell the story of your second-place science fair finish. How did that make you feel? Now imagine if that person was supposed to be your biggest fan, your partner in life, but they ignored half of everything you said. Sounds like it would hurt, a lot. To be a good partner, you have to be a good listener. A lack of communication can cause all kinds of problems in even the most loving relationships due to simple confusions about wants and needs. No one can feel loved if they don't feel understood. And if you can't hear what your partner is saying, you can't understand. Learn to listen with your whole heart. A good listener:

- cares about receiving the message clearly
- temporarily sets aside his or her own feelings
- isn't judgmental
- is truly interested in the other person's feelings and ideas
- lets them finish without interruption, eye-rolling, sighs, or discouraging facial expressions
- reflects back the speaker's point and asks if they have accurately understood

Learning to listen will be one of the most important things you do in these twelve months—for every aspect of your life, especially love. To understand and comprehend your partner, you must listen. If your man doesn't feel heard, he won't feel loved.

QUIZ: Are You a Good Listener?

Do you think you're a good listener? Find out by asking yourself the following questions.

1. Do you text or thumb through your BlackBerry in the middle of an in-person conversation?
2. Are you often on the computer while you're having a phone conversation?
3. Do you often interrupt other people's stories to tell a better one of your own?
4. Do you say things like "Hi, how are you?" or "How's it going?" while walking right past a person?
5. Do you often do things like pick at your cuticles or fiddle with the zipper of your coat to avoid making eye contact in conversation?
6. Do you talk much more about yourself than ask questions?

If you answered yes to two or more questions, you should work on your listening skills.

Love Notes

Listen up: practice good listening skills in all of your relationships, so when you find your dream mate, you'll be ready to hear what he's trying to say.

Poisonous Peeves

Is your long list of pet peeves preventing you from having a successful relationship? In the last chapter, we talked a lot about negotiation. If you had a hard time moving anything at all from your "Requirements" or "Unacceptable" column to the "Negotiable" column of your Spouse Shopping List, chances are you are letting petty issues stand in your way of happily ever after.

> **Love Notes**
> *Don't sink your own love boat with a tsunami of inconsequential annoyances.*

Anything that a man can readily change is a peeve. For example, smoking is not a pet peeve; for most, it's a deal breaker. But god-awful ties, unruly hair, keeping some rag-worthy clothes because they are comfortable, and very occasional non-ear shattering belches are pet peeves. There's not a thin line here. If the big picture is a person who makes you feel secure and happy, and meets your requirements, and a few things get on your nerves, get over it!

Your Pet Peeves

Make a list of the things that really bother you. Maybe you've called them "deal breakers" in the past.

_____

_____

_____

_____

_____

_____

_____

Now, review your list and look at how quickly you filled it out. For those of you who have come up with a lot of things that bother you very quickly, you may be a little too picky! You're looking for Mr. Right not Mr. Perfect. Remember?

Love Notes

If you absolutely cannot let go of being annoyed by a trait of your future mate, it probably won't just fade away. Address it with kindness.

If your list has more than five grievances, reduce it to just five. Now go back and see if you can apply any of this flexibility to the "Negotiable" column in your Spouse Shopping List in Chapter 2. However, if you find that these grievances are truly impossible for you to live with, don't be afraid to mention this to a potential mate. The best timing would be after he seems at least somewhat besotted with you but before you've absolutely decided on him. You need to know if he wants to please you and how flexible he is in response to requests. Try an approach such as, "You know I like/love you but I care about finishing my own sentences and I believe that you care about what I have to say." It's much more effective than "If you don't stop interrupting me when I talk, I'll find something equally annoying to do and you wouldn't like that, would you?" A habit easily changed is not synonymous with lack of integrity or values. Ask for change if you need to, but keep in mind that a peeve is a little behavior, not a whole person. And if "pet peeves" have broken up your past relationships, you need to look deeper at the real causes. Ask yourself, why are you letting these little things bother you if your big-ticket items are satisfied?

Stop Being Anchored in the Past

Being wistful for past connections that never fully materialized is like having a fridge full of moldy leftovers with no room for fresh, healthy food. When you're shopping for a relationship, there are the live ones—the ones right in front of you—and the not-so-live ones. Take your choice.

To clean up and de-clutter your love life, you may need to exorcise ghost relationships. You might fondly refer to a past partner as "the one who got away," or you may be convinced that the right person just came along at the wrong time or in the wrong place. It's easy to fall into the trap of thinking of those long-lost loves dreamily and casting them in a good light because it feels better to think about any love relationship if you don't currently have one. A relationship that wasn't right at the time might not seem so wrong when you're alone, but that doesn't mean that past relationship was perfect . . . and it doesn't even mean that it was the right relationship for you.

> ### Love Notes
> *If it's inert, it's deadwood.*
> *Date in the land of the living.*

LOVE STORIES: ANNE

After a failed short-term relationship, Anne, a broker in Chicago, was afraid to date again and instead started e-mailing her high school boyfriend, Larry, whom she hadn't seen in at least a dozen years. She had the idea in her head that Larry was the one who got away from her a long time ago and she wasn't going to let him get away again. After countless e-mails and late-night phone calls, Anne, excited and thrilled that her old love could be resurrected, booked a trip to her hometown of Normal, Ohio. She was letting her romantic fantasy convince her that she could go back to her hometown guy and maybe even her old life. But as soon as she arrived back in Normal, the truth hit her like a ton of bricks. She knew why she had left: the town and the guy were boring.

Anne learned you can't go home again. The thrill was gone. It felt like everything had happened a hundred years ago, not just twenty. While Larry enjoyed a quiet life, Anne wanted change and adventure. She had frozen Larry in time and space, and instead needed to be with a partner who matched her life in the present.

It can feel good to daydream that maybe somewhere deep-down a certain person still loves you. Maybe you did love that person so much it hurt and vice versa. But for some reason it didn't work out. If there wasn't a good reason to end the relationship, wouldn't you still be together now? And you have no idea if they could love you now or if you would even want them to. By truly knowing yourself, as we discussed in Chapter 1, you should be able to look back and have a better sense of understanding about why your past relationships didn't work for you.

> **Love Notes**
> *Love is more than just a feeling.*
> *It's an action verb.*

Fond memories can make you feel warm and fuzzy, but you're comparing reality and fantasy. By clinging to a memory, you're robbing yourself of the chance to fall in love with a real, live person instead of one who exists (perhaps inaccurately) only in your memories.

LOVE STORIES: CALLIE

After only five wonderful dates, Callie was convinced that Vincent was "the one." But after their fifth date, he began acting distant and was less interested in seeing her. On their sixth date, he abruptly ended it. Vincent's explanation was that things were complicated right now and he was not in a very good place.

Callie couldn't get him out of her mind, and was racking her brain trying to figure out what she had done to turn him off. Had she slept with him too soon? Was he repelled by her less-than-perfect body? At one point, she concluded that it was her confession of poor credit that sent him running. Needless to say, her line of thinking was not helping her current dating life. She dated other men, but was undermining herself with worry about why she had been left.

A year or so later, she ran into Vincent. He told her that when they were dating, he'd had another first (and only) date that resulted in pregnancy. Vincent's explanation of his life being "complicated" finally made sense and allowed Callie to let go of the idea that he ended things because there was something wrong with her. But, fortunately, it also made her realize she had wasted all this time pulling herself down and building him up—all based on a lack of information and her low self-confidence. She had some personal development work to do before risking another episode of stuck-in-the-past by obsessive worry about her value.

> **Love Notes**
> *People create the right time and place when they meet the right person.*

If you find that you cannot let go of a past relationship, sometimes it can help to follow your obsession. You can't make someone talk to you about the end of your relationship—and please don't try if they resist—but finding a previous date or lover is simple to do. These days, most people will turn up with a quick Facebook or Internet search. If that doesn't work, hire a detective—whatever it takes to get them out of your head. Occasionally, "the one who got away" really could be a possibility. But usually, they aren't. Either way, you can put closure on it and get on with the business of finding romantic reality.

QUIZ: Do You Want to Move Forward?

To find out if you're stuck in the past, answer the questions below.

1. **Do you want the same type of relationship you've experienced in the past?** It hasn't worked yet, has it? You need to risk the unfamiliar in order to create something wonderfully new.

2. **Are you wistful about old loves?** If so, find out if they are available and get a date with them. If they are unavailable or you are less enchanted, then stop wasting your time.

3. **Do you have one particular "type" that attracts you?** If so, you are missing out on a possible treasure by not getting past the wrapping. As I tell my students, you wouldn't take a job because of the office building!

4. **Do you only feel good about yourself in a relationship?** Savor good memories, learn from the bad ones, and let all of them go. Live not only today but in this moment, and make it good.

5. **Do you distrust unconditional love?** People who don't believe in unconditional love are not good at delivering or receiving it. If this is you, stop. Get professional help. Learning how to give and receive love is a requisite for marriage success.

Even if you've answered yes to any of the above, act on the "no" instead. Fake it until you make it. You need to get past what doesn't work for you and help create a beautiful new way of relating. Be the architect and the grateful receiver in each new relationship from this time forward.

Tips for Letting Go of Your Past

If you're having trouble moving on, take your time—you don't want to spend too much time stalling, but some recesses are necessary. Just set a reasonable deadline. A one-to-three-month plateau would be typical—any longer than that can be a bit extreme. When you feel you're ready to take the field (and have stopped comparing every new man with one from the past), you can check your progress with these steps for letting go of your past.

Put It in a Letter

Write a good-bye letter to your former love and drop it in a mailbox without an address or return address. Or, tear the letter up into tiny pieces and throw it away. You want to get your feelings out of you and into some other medium and you don't necessarily need to share them with your ex. Truthful communication with an ex can be dicey, tearful, and unnecessarily hurtful to one or both of you. And long conversations with friends can evoke their feelings instead of yours. Writing this letter is a step toward closure that you can take on your own. You can be as mean or melodramatic as you want, just get the feeling on to paper and out of your life. You'll feel better and won't have to worry about an emotionally fueled communication getting into the wrong hands and coming back to bite you some day. Trust me: a year down the road you'll thank me for not letting you mail that letter to your ex.

Emotionally De-Clutter Your Home

Do whatever you need to do to make your home feel like it's yours now, instead of a reminder of what was (whether you're remembering the good or the bad). Get rid of souvenirs of bad experiences, and keep limited memorabilia of the good. Take one object most symbolizing the relationship—whether it's a mattress on which you spent many hours making love or a kitchen tool you bought together—and dispose of it or donate it. If temporary housing is needed for some items, loan them to a friend or put in storage. The point is to keep only what helps you feel good and makes your environment less sad. If moving into a new apartment or house is an economic or geographic possibility for you, consider it. And if you need to, do it. Your home should be your haven not your hell.

Make an Honest Effort to Tie Up Loose Ends

If your life was closely interconnected with that of your ex, you need to take some time to regain your independence. Choose some moment when you are ready and put only your name on the checks, voice messages, or mailbox label, and redo your joint e-mail address or stationery. If you still have a joint bank account, close it and send him a check for half of the remaining balance. If your ex-boyfriend's mail still shows up at your apartment, file the change of address for him yourself. What else is still connecting you? Return everything that doesn't belong to you, and do it with grace and style. In the small world we live in, you never know when your paths will cross again; being able to think well of yourself and your conduct will ultimately feel sweeter than a scene or revenge.

> **Love Notes**
>
> Deep and/or lengthy love relationships require grieving, whatever the reason for the end. But someone who didn't call back after a few dates does not merit a period of mourning.

End All Stalking

Driving by someone's house or place of work, calling and hanging up, or visiting your ex's Facebook page all count as stalking. The only person you're hurting when you do these things is yourself so cut it out! Delete his number from your phone. Remove him from your instant messaging account. Adjust your Facebook settings so he'll never show up in your feed and you can't view his profile even if you try. Stop asking friends about your former love's current status—and ask them to stop telling you. If you have lots of mutual friends and you both belong to a social networking site, adjust your settings to make sure you're not updated on his goings on every time you sit down to your computer. Hanging around places you know your ex frequents also counts as stalking. People have nearly perfect radar for recognizing their former loves even from afar. Let that be a power that goes dormant in you. The only person you're hurting with your "stalking" is yourself. Every sighting or communication is a step backwards, and you need to be moving forward.

Distance Yourself

If you live in the same city, or run in the same circles as your ex and must remain friends, do so in a very distant, neutral way—but only if it's an honest neutrality. You don't want to spend your life wistful about what could have been. Plus, your future partner probably won't like the fact that you're friends with your ex. Men have unerring instinct for knowing if someone was a past lover. You can't please a partner on every front, but when it comes to former loves, if it bothers the guy you're with and you aren't an intimate friend with your ex, just wave good-bye.

Fantasize Your Anger

To move on sometimes you have to let go of any outstanding anger. To help do this, take the time to fantasize your anger. Imagine throwing your former lover off of the top of the tallest accessible building then leaving with a wonderful new lover for a romantic vacation. Once you've done that, let go of all thoughts of revenge. You'll feel better and you'll take back some room in your heart that you can give to a new partner.

Acknowledge the End

Realize that in many cases and after a suitable mourning period, it is only you who is having all of the lingering feelings. Chances are that the person you loved is probably finished with the relationship. Why aren't you? Are you hanging on to those feelings to avoid taking new risks of getting hurt? If so, take the help and support you need to realize the stakes of a bigger and better love is never going to be risk-free, so you might as well get going.

Accentuate the Positive

Focus on some fond memories and, if you can manage it, give gratitude a try. The more you dwell on how bad the relationship was or how badly your ex treated you, the more you paint yourself as a victim (even if only to yourself) and all that does is bring you down even more. Once you start to think about all the good times you had with your ex, the more you open yourself up to the possibility that you'll experience those good times again—with someone new! You'll never move on if you can't let go, so get going!

Look back at the roadblocks to love that you read about in this chapter. Which ones have you put in your own way? Write them down here, as well as any others you can think of. Let this list remind you of the behaviors you want to change.

_____

_____

_____

_____

_____

_____

_____

_____

_____

_____

_____

Once you get yourself out of a bad mental state, and stop tripping yourself up because of it, the only logical place to go is a good one. In the next chapter, you'll learn that the best thing to bring on your journey to that good place is a good attitude.

Chapter 4
Get the Right Attitude

Myth: Look great, catch a mate.
Truth: *Be* great, catch a mate.

You shouldn't think of dating in the same vein as having teeth pulled or attending a funeral. If you are dreading the experience, you're the one bringing the doom to the room. If you're not excited by the idea of dating, it's time to up the thrill level and look forward to dating with an attitude of eager anticipation. Allow yourself to see each date for what it really is: the beginning of many limitless possibilities or at least another of the numbers you have to run to find your partner. The experience is supposed to be fun—and so are you!

Luckily, pleasant and productive dating is simple and anyone can do it. You just have to be willing to take along someone you really like—you!—and focus on bringing out the very best in every date before you decide if he has passed or failed. If the other person takes the pass before you do, realize that they just saved you from dragging on with something that was not going to work anyway. In this chapter, you'll learn how to be the best—and most positive—woman that you can be!

Build Confidence and Self-Worth

How can you expect anyone else to love you if you don't love yourself? Building confidence and self-worth is by far the hardest and most complicated part of adjusting your attitude, but it's also the most rewarding. If you can do it for yourself, improving your mental health won't be a draining job left to your mate. You want him to focus on loving you and enjoying you, not struggling to love you enough to make up for the fact that you don't love yourself.

LOVE STORIES: EDIE

Edie, a thirty-one-year-old, good-looking architect, was confident in her abilities, and so was everyone else. She was always being sought out for important projects because she was good and was easily able to sell her talent to prospective clients. But when it came to Edie's personal life, there was zero demand for her—she had no draw. That's because as far as she was concerned, all of her value was in her résumé. Her professional confidence was sky-high, but her self-esteem was low. Edie had no doubt that she was the perfect person to design the new headquarters for a high-dollar corporation, but was not able to convince herself that she had anything to offer in a romantic relationship.

After months of therapy, Edie began to see that she was more than just the girl her father used to alternately criticize or ignore and continually discount and disparage. She realized she was putting all of her effort toward accomplishments in order to prove her father wrong and was hiding her feelings behind a résumé. (When you've spent a childhood with abuse, love doesn't feel safe.) First she had to accept and love the child she was, then appreciate the woman she had become. She was successful, and also caring, loving, and funny. Once she truly believed in herself, it began to show. She became more connected: spending more time with people socially instead of being overinvolved with accomplishments, and she self-assigned a new project—dating. Eventually, the demand for Edie as a date was nearly as high as the demand for Edie as an architect.

The Law of Attraction

Think back to a time you've gone to a restaurant, and asked the waiter how the pasta of the day is. If he responds, "Um, yeah, it's good, I think; people seem to like it," there's a good chance you'll say, "I'll have the burger." But if he excitedly relays how he's had it three times and each time it's been fantastic—"The flavor of the caramelized onions really pops. You won't be disappointed!"—you're much more likely to say, "Great, sold!"

> ## Love Notes
> *If you date with a low sense of self-worth, you are likely to end up in a relationship that's not worth your while.*

If you're going to sell yourself as a potential spouse, you need to be as knowledgeable and confident in yourself as the waiter was in the pasta of the day. Trying to convince someone to date you when you're not confident in your product (you!) will decidedly damage your credibility. In a relationship where neither person really values him or herself as a human being, it's common for one or both partners to become insecure and defensive and unable to share their own needs with the other person. That lack of communication can lead to insecurity about one's self and the relationship, arguments, deceptive behavior, and neediness—which, in turn, contributes to an even lower sense of self-esteem. It can turn into a big Catch-22 that you don't want to be a part of.

People choose mates whose self-esteem matches their own. So now is the time to raise your own confidence level if need be. When you're confident, you go into a relationship valuing yourself and your own feelings and have faith in the strength of your marriage, so it's much easier to say to your partner, "I need more time with you," or "What you said to me at dinner last night really hurt my feelings and here's why." After all, when you're in a relationship with a man you love, you shouldn't be afraid to speak your mind.

LOVE STORIES: DIANA

Paul was the perfect guy—on paper. His résumé was outstanding, but he was chronically, almost pathologically immature. He came off like Superman but needed constant assurance to keep him from reverting to an insecure Clark Kent. His fiancée, Diana, had extremely low self-confidence and felt lucky to have someone who wanted her in his life. She was a sheep in sheep's clothing. She catered to his whims and met all of his needs without much joy, figuring it was a small price to pay for the lifestyle he provided her in return.

But the further they got into the relationship, they both began to realize that what looked like a good deal, wasn't. By having his almost infantile self-indulgence indulged at home, Paul's immaturity began to show on the job. And although Diana had financial security, being with Paul didn't make her feel any better about herself. They stayed together, but major work was required on both their parts to keep the relationship afloat. It was a high-maintenance relationship then and three years later, it still is.

Learn to Love Your Body

I remember seeing a cartoon titled "The Difference Between Women & Men" that had a naked man and woman each looking into a full-length mirror. The thin woman saw a woman about three times bigger looking back at her, while the overweight, balding man saw a chiseled Adonis in his reflection. While some men are uncomfortable with their looks, body image issues are especially common for women.

Love Notes
By the time a man sees you naked, he already desires you and is more focused on enjoying than judging.

Fortunately, the person who loves you will also love your body—it is part of you, after all. And the good news is that men don't see you in the critical way you see yourself. Men are more like impressionists; they see a beautiful picture and are a little fuzzy on the details. They are turned on by your shape and hate it if you start pointing out your faults because it mars their picture of you. Stand naked in front of your mirror and find one lovely feature about your body—hair, eyes, lips, it doesn't matter. But naked or not, when you look in any mirror, don't walk away without taking a positive image with you. It is your perception of reality that may be damaging your confidence level, and your view is not necessarily reality. Consider what Robert De Niro reportedly once said, "According to a new survey, women say they feel more comfortable undressing in front of men than they do undressing in front of other women. They say that women are too judgmental, where, of course, men are just grateful."

Be Good to Your Body

Learning to love yourself is the best beauty tip of all. You have no legitimate excuse for not practicing self-care and packaging your true self in an attractive exterior. Unfortunately, many women take care of their homes, pets, and everyone around them at the expense of caring for their own bodies and even health. But the truth is that the way you look and carry yourself cannot only affect your attitude, it also sends a message to potential dates about your interest level.

It's instinctual to put effort into looking good. And it's instinctual to notice someone making effort to attract. Most animals preen and clean to make sure their fur is sleek and unmatted. Among animals, looking unkempt and with patchy fur is a sign the animal is diseased or dying, and others shun her. Not so different with humans. Unclean hair and frumpy clothing is unlikely to communicate a dire disease, but it certainly doesn't draw anyone to you either. You want potential mates to see you as full of life and ready to date. When you look your best, you are giving yourself your best chance to attract dates, but even more importantly you will feel better about yourself.

> ### Love Notes
> *You are not going to attract someone from across the room with your inner self.*

You've likely seen those shampoo commercials in which a woman has a shiny new hairstyle and walks down the street like a supermodel, stopping traffic and turning all heads. Sure, they're exaggerations of the real world, but the truth is, when you make a little change it can really boost your confidence, even if it's temporary. When you look good, you feel good. And when you feel good, people are drawn to you.

Exercise

Exercise is a health essential with proven capacity to improve your immune system and prevent disease. In addition to making your body look great, the mental, emotional, and social benefits should be enough to get you up and out of the house or in front of a yoga or aerobics DVD. These benefits are numerous:

> ### Love Notes
> *Put this on your calendar: get up, get out, and do something—anything.*

- Setting and reaching even small goals, like running for ten minutes without stopping, can help you gain confidence, and increases perception of shape even if no change has occurred.
- Working out releases endorphins, the feel-good brain chemicals.
- Joining a running or hiking group, or a recreational sports league, is a great way to meet new people (including potential dates and date-hunting buddies).
- Numerous studies have shown that exercise increases sex drive—some say up to 100 percent. You may not want or be able to use that now, but hopefully you will.

So get to it! You don't need to sign up for a marathon tomorrow, or even a half marathon. But small changes to your activity level can mean big changes to mood and attitude. An evening walk three times a week, parking at the farthest corner of parking lots when you go shopping, or signing up for a group fitness class—any motion beats being sedentary. If you're worried you won't stick with it, pick something you really like and do it with people you enjoy.

Bottoms Up

Drinking eight glasses of water a day is good for more than just your health. Everybody feels better when they're hydrated, and getting plenty of fluids is also great for your skin, hair, and plumbing. If that's not reason enough: dehydration can cause bad breath, and that's the last thing you need while dating.

> ### Love Notes
> *Dehydration makes you cranky, is bad for your complexion, and can make you overly hungry. Drink your daily eight glasses of eight ounces of water.*

Nutrition

What you do and don't put into your body every day can have a huge impact on your mood. While foods like chocolate and pasta can give you immediate and short-lived feelings of satisfaction, too much of anything can make you feel groggy and grumpy in the long run. Proteins, fruits and vegetables, and fewer simple carbohydrates will give you more energy. And if you don't already, take a multivitamin that's appropriate for your age and medical condition. Healthy habits started at any age contribute to overall quality of life. They are also great for keeping a healthy attitude, a positive interest in sex, and the clear eyes and fresh skin that keep you looking and feeling attractive.

Accentuate the Positive; Eliminate the Negative

A quick return to positivism may be your—or any single girl's—most important asset. No matter how physically attractive, charming, or intelligent you are, if you see someone who's "un-datable" or "meant to be alone" when you look in the mirror, other people will see you that way, too. Instead of wallowing about what you think is wrong with you, catch those unruly negative thoughts and flip the switch to positives. It is an art. Just try it.

> ## Love Notes
> *Whether you like it or not, you are what you eat—and you look like it, too. So eat mostly fresh, healthy foods that satisfy you, and eat only when you are hungry.*

We're already asked the question, "How can you expect anyone to love you if you don't love yourself?" Well, the same goes for attraction. Have you ever had a friend who you didn't necessarily find attractive, but men couldn't seem to keep their eyes off of her? Consider her attitude. How much time did she spend talking about what was wrong with her body, skin, clothes or hair? Probably little to none. When someone loves herself, and loves life, people are drawn to her, even if she's not conventionally attractive. People want to enjoy life with someone who so clearly already enjoys it herself. That is human nature.

LOVE STORIES: ALLISON

Allison was a website designer. The kind of girl everyone liked. She had a lot of friends and was always going out and meeting new people, including single men. But after several seemingly promising relationships failed to take flight, somewhere in her mid-twenties, she convinced herself that she was "meant to be alone."

By her late twenties, what was an easy way to dismiss the pain and disappointment of failed relationships had become protection from having any at all. She had stopped taking any chances when it came to romance. That is, until a friend pointed out that it didn't make any sense at all for Allison—

a woman who was spiritual but did not believe in God or divine intervention—to think that there was someone in the sky choreographing her life and making sure she would always be alone. "How self-centered of me," she admitted later, "to think that there was some universal force working nonstop to keep me single."

Once her own sensibilities forced her to look at what was really keeping her from meeting and making a go of it with the right person—her fear of risk taking—she declared a new start. Allison took her mind off her past and changed her attitude toward dating to "let's move ahead and make it work for me."

Forgive Your Own Mistakes, and Learn from Them

Everyone makes mistakes. Everyone. Luckily, your character is not measured by the mistakes you've made, but by how you've handled them. If you can accept that you will be making mistakes, and then learn from them and move on, you'll be much better off not only in your dating life, but in all other areas as well. After all, if you beat yourself up every time you make a mistake in life or love and strive for perfection (remember what we talked about in Chapter 3: perfectionism is boring!), you're going to have a hard time growing as a person. So you went on a few too many dates with the wrong person? Learn how to sort faster. You wore an unflattering dress on a first date? Pick one winning outfit to wear every first date. You got into a fight with a friend? Be the bigger person and apologize. Even years spent in a bad relationship can be turned into something positive: they probably made you damn sure of what you don't want out of your next one. So go easy on yourself. You give forgiveness to others; it's high time you grant it to yourself as well.

Fight Fear

Fear paralyzes, and in romantic relationships, most fears originate from a fear of abandonment or rejection: *when he gets to know the real me, he will leave.* But it's fear that can keep you from the very person who *won't* disappoint you. Fear of rejection or abandonment can play out before you even have your first phone call or walk through a door, and it can stay through a relationship and even marriage. It breeds distrust and insecurities, in turn ruining what could otherwise be a happy partnership. You can conquer your fears. Give it a try with the following fear busters.

- **Pinpoint the origin of your fear.** You might not be able to identify exactly what planted the seed of fear in you, but if you think really hard, you probably have some idea. Most people think fear of rejection or abandonment comes from an early romantic heartbreak, but it usually goes deeper, like parental divorce or the death of a loved one at a young age.
- **Wrestle with your fear.** If you can, talk to the person who disappointed you. Try to work out the feelings that you're still carrying around. If you need to, talk to a counselor or therapist to work though the original pain.
- **Don't blame people for others' mistakes.** Your new boyfriend is not your dad and he won't disappoint you in the same ways—especially if you're making a point of not dating people who resemble your parents in personality as we discussed in Chapter 1.
- **Work on your self-image.** People with a fear of abandonment have to fight a lot harder to truly believe they're a prize and worthy of unconditional love. If you have a lot of fear, you might need to put a pause on dating to spend extra time working on building your confidence and self-worth. And that's okay.
- **Be brave.** When you recognize fear for what it is, you can make a concerted effort to go outside your comfort zone and take a

calculated risk. Once you have realized the source of pain, faced the people who caused it if necessary, been willing to close the door on your past, and are brave enough to go on despite it, your fear will slowly but surely melt away.

It's true that the only thing you have to fear is fear itself. Get past the fear, and you'll find that the things that you think caused that fear probably aren't that bad. And even if they are, they're in the past; how can they hurt you now unless you allow it?

Have a Great Support System

As you learned in the last chapter, it's critically important to eliminate both negativism and people who spread it and to surround yourself with people who support you in your marriage goals. A quick way to find out who's an asset and who's not is to tell everyone you know that you're reading this book about finding your dream mate in a year. Consider reducing contact with anyone who doesn't respond with enthusiasm to your goal. It's a lot like the Olympics. If you were training and your friends or family told you that you didn't stand a chance of winning, your coach would put you in seclusion to keep you as far away from them as possible.

LOVE STORIES: CHANDRA

Chandra and her friend Julie listened to each other's problems, but 98 percent of the time it went one way because Julie had the winning disasters both in frequency and drama levels. Chandra spent some time tallying up the time she spent either talking to Julie or worrying about Julie and she found Julie was taking up too much of her headspace and too much time—and it didn't look like it was ever going to change. Julie depleted Chandra's energy and left her too exhausted to capitalize on all of her dating opportunities. It was difficult, but Chandra decided to end this one-way friendship and make her search for true love a priority in her life. She's now successfully dating the man of her dreams.

You need to see less of the people in your life who have a pitying or hopeless view of you. Instead of talking to them five days a week, talk to them just twice a week. Unsure of who's really a negative influence? After a phone call with certain friends and family members, do you feel better or worse? If you feel worse, cut the cord or make it longer. It's amazing what a relief it will be and how much less of a burden you'll feel when those people's negativity is either expunged or minimalized.

> ## Love Notes
> You'll be surprised at how your spirits soar when you spend even thirty fewer minutes a week with someone's who's negative.

Self-Market Based on Your Assets, Not Your Faults

It's true, everyone has faults, but that simple fact doesn't mean you can't find a good guy who will love you for you. Approach your "faults" as challenges you intend to overcome or simply as something that might not be a good match for a certain type of partner, so they can stop being recurring "reasons" for your dating failure. Instead of focusing on the negative, take the time to recognize and appreciate your own strengths as a person. Do not reveal any downside early on. Any perceived flaw can be reformulated. For example, if you don't have much formal education then just state what you do have, your other means of learning, and what you've accomplished. Speak of yourself with pride and don't be afraid to discuss your ambitions if you have them. Dating is shopping and your sales pitch has to be focused on your assets and how to best reveal your sweetness, listening skills, story telling, or great relationships with family and friends. Remember, to understand your power, it's important to realistically determine what you are bringing to the table and to have a good understanding of your own "market value." Take some time to focus on your strong points.

My Strong Points Notepad

When you're trying to focus on your strong points, it can help to make a list of your assets and your desirable and admirable traits. For example:

Assets	Desirable/Admirable Traits
healthy lifestyle	sexy/sensual
good and honest person	positive
fun loving	intelligent
great listener	good body
socially adept	pretty smile
spiritual	honest
ambitious	trustworthy

Make your own list here:

Assets	Desirable/Admirable Traits

Once you've created your list, ask one or two of your friends to give you their answers and add them to your list. Keep this with you as a reminder whenever you are being self-critical. In addition, pull out your list the next time you're feeling un-datable. Read it as many times as you need to until you've convinced yourself that any man would be lucky to have you as part of his life. Once you can pinpoint what it is that you really have to offer to someone and contribute to a relationship, finding a good match is so much easier.

LOVE STORIES: ELAINE

Elaine had been emotionally buffeted by dating, but always willing to try again because she was determined to get married before her younger sister beat her to the altar.

Elaine came to my office after what she called "59 painfully blind dates." And she wasn't exaggerating. One man had patted her hand and said he hoped she got married soon because he just didn't think she should be out in the world alone. Elaine knew something was going wrong—she was looking for love and instead was only finding sympathy—but she didn't realize that her "little girl" defense mechanism might get her adopted but wasn't helping her get married. She needed to change her attitude, but first she needed to see the image she was projecting into the world and which of her more positive traits she should focus on. Soon she came to realize that she had a natural demureness that was potentially appealing to many men. Once she realized how to work that—as more of a steel magnolia than wilting violet—she met someone who liked taking care of women. Her sweetness and naïveté attracted him big-time. They made an instant connection, and Elaine recognized that her "weakness" was a strong point for him.

Reformulate Your Way of Thinking about Yourself

An easy way to sell yourself based on your strong points is to simply reformulate your thinking. It's as easy as flipping a mental switch, but it takes practice.

Never been married? No matter your age, it just means you carry around that much less extra baggage. Really! Think about this: no one else has ever affected your credit score, you don't write an alimony check every month, and your future spouse will never have to live up to the idea of being better than your ex.

Divorced? If you're divorced, not only is this your opportunity for an upgrade, you'll also go into your next committed relationship with experience and realistic expectations of a successful partnership. You've been through the good and the bad, and you're stronger and more emotionally educated because of it. You know what works for you and what doesn't, and you can be confident in that knowledge.

Widowed? Widows and widowers are often perceived as still being in love, but what a widowed person may have to offer is proof of a successful relationship. As long as you are not making them even better over time and don't build your deceased spouse into every conversation and every thought, you will simply be perceived as someone who's good at marriage.

> **Love Notes**
> *Your glass is half-full (or overflowing) if you believe it is. See yourself that way and sell yourself that way.*

A single parent? You may feel that your children are blocking your attempts to find a mate. But they can be an asset in your search for love. Remember: you're not looking for the perfect man, you're looking for the perfect man *for you*. Shop for the dream mate who wants the whole package—including stepchildren. And the fact that you raised children (especially if they turned out well) just goes to show your future partner what a great nurturer you are.

Be Enthusiastic and Interesting

You would let a potential boss know that you're excited about a job, so why wouldn't you do the same with a potential mate? Acting uninterested or unenthusiastic about a man isn't usually a turn-on. The man who wants a serious relationship isn't going to waste time playing games with a woman who doesn't appear interested. So if you like someone, let him know!

Somewhere along the line, a rule got made that men should wait three days before calling to ask for a date. It's time to kick that rule to the curb! The man who calls the next day and says, "I'd love to see you again," gets big points for being enthusiastic. And you shouldn't be afraid to enthusiastically accept and greet your date with a smile that conveys you're delighted to be with him.

> ## Love Notes
> *Enthusiasm is contagious.*
> *If you have it, others will want to catch it.*

And do let your enthusiasm spill over into the rest of your life. See every date, meeting, or event as an opportunity for adventure. This doesn't mean you have to give up all cynicism, send a thank-you card after every date, or carry around a kazoo just in case the moment strikes you; just don't curb your enthusiasm.

Become Charming and Accepting

You probably know someone who's naturally charming—a person you're drawn to, someone you want to be around and talk to until the sun comes up. For others, charm doesn't come so easily. Luckily, you're not born with charm; it is made and you can learn what to do by following the advice below.

Smile, Smile, Smile

For both men and women, smiling is an extremely important communication tool. It says, "I'm safe, I'm friendly, you can come meet me." If you're not good at smiling, or you think you may be an awkward smiler, practice on your furniture, move on to pets, and then strangers on the street (except, of course, the creepy or dangerous ones). Then start beaming at the men who interest you.

Listen, Really Listen

Being a good listener is a huge part of being charming. Why would anyone want to have a conversation with someone who's not really listening to what they have to say? If you need to, go back and review what makes a good listener in Chapter 3. Even if you're still working on your conversation skills, this is one area where you can most definitely fake it 'til you make it: just ask lots of questions to show care and concern and remark on their answers. Then get out there and practice on everyone you meet.

> ### Love Notes
> *The better you understand the other person's perspective, the more pleasant any interaction will be.*

Learn More

Chances are, you're an expert on something, so as long as you're not attacking anyone with your politics or any extremist views, don't be afraid to talk about what you know and love. But in order to date within a large pool, you need to be well versed on a wide variety of subjects including current events, politics, economics, music, etc. Read blogs, newspapers, magazines, or whatever medium you're most comfortable with, daily. While you certainly don't need to be an expert on every subject, you should be able to hold your own at a party or a dinner table to at least give the impression that you have some idea of what's going on in the world. Never stop learning. You want to be interesting to talk to on the first date, the second date, the twentieth date, and twenty years down the road.

Cooperate

By now you have probably noticed that life doesn't always go the way you want it to, and unfair happens. So, you have two options: you can either pout and make sure everyone knows when you don't get your way, or you can choose to go with the flow and make the best of the situations presented to you. Which person would you rather date? Exactly!

Be Accepting

You know what's not charming? Rejecting everyone who crosses your path. Saying no all the time doesn't make you a hot commodity; it makes you intimidating and unapproachable. Remember that people who look great at first glance can disappoint you and someone you might not be immediately drawn to can surprise you. Cast a wide net. You never know what hidden treasures are waiting for you in the wide world of dating.

> **Love Notes**
> *Caution: Rough doesn't always have a diamond inside. If a diamond doesn't emerge with minor excavation, stop mining.*

Make Others Feel Good

When others feel good about being around you, consider yourself to be successfully charming. One way to charm is to be prepared with topics of conversation. Be complimentary, friendly, kind, polite, and culturally literate. Keep a Charmers' Resource List to help you build your repertoire. There are some suggestions below, but feel free to add to this as you find things that work for you.

Charmers' Resource List
- Know daily news (for conversation topics)
- Exercise regularly (endorphins make you happy)
- Read sports pages (to at least know who won and who lost)
- Compliment everyone you meet (it's possible)
- Accept compliments with a "thank you" (not a self-disparaging retort)
- Cook (it's one of the ways to a man's heart)
- Make sure that every first date you want to see again knows it
- Learn to dance (a very acceptable and romantic way to find out if you're comfortable being close)
- _____
- _____
- _____
- _____

Let Your Goals Be Your Guide

I'll let you in on a secret: people without any dreams, goals, or aspirations aren't charming or interesting. If you've ever met someone who has completely given up wanting anything more for her future, you know that those people are not very much fun to be around. They lower the energy level in the room and are likely to be dating challenged as well.

> **Love Notes**
> *Change happens with or without you.*
> *You might as well participate.*

It's important to be happy with yourself and your life and your choices. But if you felt entirely satisfied, you probably wouldn't be reading this book. Personal growth in some form or at least healthy curiosity should happen until the day you die. Isn't life more interesting imagining what you wish for your future and looking forward to change? Keep growing and dreaming, and before you know it, you'll find that you're realized some—if not all—of your dreams!

Goals

In the first chapter, you reflected on the last year of your life, and forgave yourself for choices or actions you weren't proud of. Now it's time to set some goals for the year ahead. Answer the following questions as they pertain to only the next twelve months of your life.

In the next year . . .

If you could make only three changes, what would they be? _____
_____

Is there anyone you wish to treat differently? _____
_____

Are there confrontations you wish to have or conflicts you want to resolve? _____
_____

What do you want to achieve emotionally? _____
_____

What do you want to achieve professionally? _____
_____

What do you want to do more of? _____
_____

If you accomplish only two things, what will they be? _____
_____

What do you want to change about your home and your personal space? _____
_____

Is there a habit you want to break? _____
_____

What crazy or different experience would you like to have? _____
_____

How will you be more creative? _____
_____

Are there ways you want to grow spiritually (whether faith-based or not)? _____

What boundaries are you going to set? _____
_____

How can you be more romantic or draw more romance into your life? _____

Overall, how will you be more loving and compassionate? _____
_____

What are three words that define your intention for this year? _____
_____
_____

Keep your answers in mind and review your goals every one to two months. Some you'll keep to yourself, and others you'll share with friends, family, and maybe even potential mates. When you accomplish one of them, congratulate yourself.

Every chapter in this book is about making positive changes. Let your success with each step help you move on to the next with more confidence and excitement and be dedicated to feeling good as well as being successful at finding your mate. The next step here is to learn how to de-stress dating—something you'll soon be able to embrace with confidence!

Chapter 5

Stress-Proof Your Dating Life

Myth: Dating is stressful.
Truth: Dating is only stressful if your life is stressful.

Stress can ruin your dating life or keep you from having one at all. People under stress have a shorter fuse and little patience, and stress impedes your ability to meet and recognize potential soul mates; it may cause you to quickly rule out a potential mate based on instant judgments. Singles under stress tend to make too many negative assumptions such as "there are no good men," or "no one's relationship is really happy." Clearly these blanket beliefs can only get in the way of finding your perfect match. Fortunately, it is possible to stress-proof your dating life. Keep reading to find out what you can do to bring some peace into your soul mate search.

QUIZ: Are You Suffering from Dating Stress?

Before you can successfully tackle your quest to meet your dream mate, you should have an idea of how much of a hold stress has on your dating life—or lack thereof—and take the steps necessary to overcome it. Answer yes or no to the following questions to see how much stress affects you.

1. Are you scared or tense about dating?
2. Do you discourage other singles' efforts to meet you?
3. Do you work or date hard with no breaks?

4. Are you not enjoying dates because you're distracted or worried about other parts of your life?
5. Are you having trouble saying no to dead-end dates?
6. Is your diet, exercise regimen, and sleep pattern not what they should be?
7. Do you criticize yourself and your dates often?
8. Do you spend more time doing what you don't want to rather than what you'd like to be doing?
9. Are you worried that if you start dating you won't be able to get your work, housecleaning, _____ (fill in the blank) done?
10. Do you feel like your house, car, desk, etc., is a mess?

Three or more yes answers means that you need to pause and take care of you. Return to dating when you can enjoy it. Having fun helps lower your stress level!

Reduce Stress

Even if the quiz indicates you're not suffering from too much dating stress, there's probably at least one source of stress in your life—and for most people, there's more than one. Dating is less stressful if life in general is less stressful. Look back at the Personal Data Form in Chapter 1. What areas of life are stressful to you right now? Consider the following parts of your life. Are they stressing you out and keeping you from finding the perfect guy?

Work

Work can get in the way of looking for a mate, and work actually used to be an excuse that no one would argue with. But even today, people have what seem like valid reasons for working too much: cutbacks have forced fewer employees to do more, they're starting their own businesses, etc. More often, work can slowly sneak up on you until it's completely invaded your life and one day you wake up a workaholic: answering business related e-mails as they come in, even on evenings and weekends, and taking calls from the boss at every hour of the day and night. While there may be times you're legitimately on call and need to deal with a crisis, nobody is important enough that they need to work 24/7. But watch out for people who are seduced into believing they are; for commitment-phobes, winning at work is a great cover for being worried about losing at love.

> ## Love Notes
> *No one is going to marry you to be alone. If you're serious about getting married, you need to get serious about your work/life balance starting now.*

If work is a big area of stress in your life, ask yourself this: *Am I working too much because my job depends on it, or by choice?* If it's the former, maybe it's time to look for a new job. If it's the latter, think about whether you will need to sacrifice some work time to have time for getting married this year. It's not unreasonable to tell your boss that you're going to cut back on evening and weekend work so you'll perform better at the office during the week, or to set up an automatic e-mail vacation response on the weekends, letting people know you'll get back to them on Monday morning.

Friends and Family

As we've discussed, friends and family can be your best support team—or a hindrance to your search for your dream mate. They may think they have your best interests at heart, but some of them might have a hidden agenda to keep you all to themselves.

You're making major changes in your life in preparation for marrying your dream mate, so make sure you're not holding on to anything that can hold you back, like a really crazy friend. People tend to keep "frenemies" because it's more comfortable than breaking up with them, or because having difficult friends around feels normal to you. It's a pretty common experience to have some sort of dysfunction in life, and keeping someone around to carry on that dysfunction can become a habit—a stressful one. At this point, you should have already put some distance between yourself and less-supportive "friends." And if you haven't, you may find that soon you're so involved in your exciting new dating life that some of them fall along the wayside, anyway.

> ### Love Notes
> *If the friendship is heavy on work or guilt and light on reward, re-evaluate the relationship. Good friends make your life better, not worse.*

Great friends are valuable assets—they'll give you all the support they can and do their best to help you reduce your stress levels—and they are a great dowry. Conversely, if you're going after a wonderful, healthy mate, he isn't going to want to deal with your collection of destructive, unsupportive people.

Parents

Parents can be your best support or your greatest stress provokers. When you're young, your parents may put pressure on you to succeed and may set the rules you rebel against. When your parents are old, you may have the responsibility of parenting them. Unfortunately, in some families, there might be a parent or parents who want you to stay single so they can keep you all to themselves—just like a selfish, insecure friend might do. Rather than giving in, be strong, and make the decisions that are best for you. Is your mother's mandatory Friday-night dinner really more important than your quest to find your dream mate? The answer is definitely no—at least for this year.

Even if you spend less time with your parents as you focus more time on yourself and your new dating life, they're still your parents, and most of the time, you're still going to have to deal with them on some level. The key to a successful relationship with one or both of your parents is negotiating a relationship with them on an adult-to-adult basis that you can all live with. If you can do this, the better you'll be able to handle the stresses and joys that parents can bring.

> ## Love Notes
> *You can't change your parents, but you can change the way you react to them.*

Children

While the joys of raising a child can be the best thing in your life, raising kids can make you feel overworked and underappreciated. If you're a single parent, that stress is often doubled—and if you don't manage your time and relationships well, your stress can intensify when you're trying to date.

If you're choosing a mate who's a good match for you, he needs to be aware and very accepting of your children. If your children are stressful for you or your mate, they're going to be a stress on your relationship, so deal with the stress now before it's amplified.

> ## Love Notes
> *You need to listen to your children's input, not accept their dominance.*

Children can be resistant to change, especially after a divorce or death of a parent. Even when change is for the best, they may dig in their heels, objecting to any of your attempts at a new life. Being a parent means making decisions that benefit all of you. Their opinions should be acknowledged and appreciated, but your children are not the decision-makers.

However, in some cases, it's the parent who's resistant to change. Sometimes parents hide behind their children because they're afraid of taking a new romantic risk. Some single parents—especially those with only one child—inhibit their wish for a real, adult relationship by establishing an exclusive emotional bond with their child. If this sounds like you, you might be putting off the search for a mate, thinking that the love of your child is all you need. That kind of love may feel safer than the uncertain hot-and-cold love of a romantic partner and peer, but when it comes right down to it, it's unhealthy for yourchild and for you.

> ## Love Notes
> While your child's sense of security should be your priority, be careful you're not using it as an excuse for avoiding the risks of loving a grownup.

Whatever your relationship to your children is, do yourself *and* them a favor by making stress-proof dating a priority in your life *right now* by taking the following steps:

1. Talk to your children as honestly as you need to about your new dating life. If they're younger, explain to them that you're going out because you are a person who needs to have fun and play with your friends, just like kids do, and dating is a way to have fun and to meet someone new. If they're older, they should be able to understand your need for a partner, even if they don't like it at first.

2. Don't introduce your children to casual dates. The only appropriate time to introduce your children is when you've established that he is an eligible person and the interest is mutual. When that time comes, your children don't have to accept your new mate right away, but they do need to know that treating anyone you bring into the home with courtesy and respect is their *only* option.

3. While the care of your children is extremely important, you don't have to do it alone. If your plate is too full, it's okay (and important) to ask for help. Ask your friends and family for help, and get in touch with other parents to arrange carpools.

> ## Love Notes
> *Overworking the role of parent doesn't make you a better mother—it makes you tired. Do yourself and your children a favor and ask for help when you need it.*

4. If you have young children, do all you can to find at least one great babysitter you can afford. If you don't have a babysitter, ask your friends and family to help, or look into a babysitting share with other parents. Be sure you are comfortable that the kids are safe with the sitter you choose and know that your children might at first be resistant to the idea, but they'll get used to it. Children are adaptable, and it's important that they learn that you are not 100 percent available.

If the idea of putting aside your duties as a parent a few hours a week to date still fills you with guilt or fear, remember this: children aren't always reasonable, but they are highly impressionable; when they see you taking care of your own well-being, they will be able to follow this healthy model themselves in years to come.

Sex

If sex causes a lot of stress for you, look to your past for clues. Go back to your first sexual experiences and look at the patterns of what pleased or displeased you. For women, especially, sex works better within the security of a committed relationship. If you're not currently in one, that could be the source of your problem. For the most part, women want to feel desired and affirmed in order to bring out the best of their sexuality. If sex is only great for you with forbidden relationships (a married partner perhaps), then you need to focus on building your way back to intimacy with available people. By remembering your goal of marriage, and allowing it to motivate your feelings and give you strength, you can change your attractions from unavailable men to single men who are ready and waiting—for you!

> ### Love Notes
> *If mama ain't happy . . . Being a happy, well-rounded parent is a big part of raising happy, healthy children.*

If the mere idea of sex stresses you out, ask yourself why. If you're insecure about your body, go back and heed the advice given in the "Learn to Love Your Body" section of Chapter 4. If you're worried that you're not experienced enough when it comes to sex, there are plenty of books and informational articles at the library and online. If you have deeper sexual wounds stemming from some abuse in your past, definitely see a therapist or counselor. Many issues (trust for one) may need to be worked out before an exciting and free sexual relationship is possible for you. No-sex marriages, generally defined as six times a year or less, more frequently have an atmosphere of tension. Sex may not be everything but it can sure provide the juice.

Fear

Fear is a huge source of stress for many women. For some, social anxiety prohibits them from meeting new people or even carrying on simple conversations with strangers. For others, a fear of intimacy keeps them from getting close to anyone. Fear of abandonment or fear of commitment can lead you to choose the wrong partner over and over and over again. Fear symptoms include: self-pity, herd behavior (traveling in groups may make you more comfortable but a lot less approachable), chronic martyrdom or complaining, feeling overwhelmed, withdrawing from a relationship before asking for what you want and giving the other person a chance to change, or grabbing a "right now" choice instead of being able to wait for the right one.

Fear can be detrimental to more than your relationships, though; it can also damage your mind and body. If fear is a major source of stress for you, go back to Chapter 4 and read the section "Fight Fear." Read it as many times as you need to until you believe you can look fear in the eye and then march right over it on your path to a successful, committed relationship. Practice fighting fear in every area of your life, every day. If your fears are debilitating, talk to a therapist—there could be a way, and a possibly easy way, to treat it. You'd see a doctor if you had some sort of skin trouble that wouldn't go away, and you need to apply the same care and concern to your emotions.

Your Past Loves

Your best love experience might be the one you hold all others up to. And your worst love experience might have left you wary of all romantic relationships. Over time, memories may make the divorced spouse worse than he really was, and memories may idealize the spouse of the widowed. That's why ghostbusting (Chapter 3) is so important. A new relationship isn't going to be exactly like your best one or your worst one. It will be wonderful and rewarding or terrible in completely new ways. But if you've been doing the personal work suggested in this book, at this point someone like an undesirable former love wouldn't fit into your life the way a new person (who's a good match) will. So stop worrying about trying to find the right person for you and just let it happen.

Your Current Romance

This book is all about developing and maintaining a committed relationship with the best person for you, and at this point you have already worked through an amazing amount of information about yourself and your relationships with others. If a current relationship is causing you stress, that doesn't mean it's doomed, but you might need to take a few steps back, empty your baggage, and repack for the relationship you want and need. In doing so, you might find that the person you're seeing is not the person you really want to travel through life with or that they look better when you are less stressed.

Only you can know for sure if the person you're seeing is the one with which you want to establish a loving, marriage-worthy relationship, but take the quiz below to aid in your decision. Similar to the two Be Honest with Yourself quizzes in the first chapter, this quiz can help you to determine whether you're being honest with yourself and realistic about a future with your current mate.

QUIZ: Is Your Current Mate a Good Match for You?

Take this quiz to help determine if your current mate or date is your best choice.

1. Looking back at your Love Résumé in Chapter 1, would you say your current relationship possesses:
   A. more of your healthy patterns?
   B. more of your unhealthy patterns?

2. Looking back at your Spouse Shopping List in Chapter 2, would you say that your current mate has:
   A. most of what you want in a lifelong partner?
   B. little of what you want in a lifelong partner?

3. Would you say that your date or mate:
   A. feels lucky to have you?
   B. thinks that you're lucky to have him?
   C. feels that you're both lucky for having each other (with a leaning toward feeling like the luckier one)?

4. Does your current mate:
   A. share your desire to eventually enter into a lifelong, committed relationship?

B. not share your desire to enter into a lifelong, committed relationship?

C. you're not sure.

5. If you're naked or sexually intimate with your mate, do you feel:

   A. secure, happy, turned on?

   B. insecure and nervous?

6. Do you and your current mate:

   A. mostly agree on the big things like love, money, and sex?

   B. disagree about love, money, and sex?

   C. you haven't talked about it.

7. If your mate found this book on your shelf, he would most likely:

   A. be curious but probably see it as a positive step for your relationship.

   B. run away as fast as he can.

   C. get upset or make fun of you.

If you answered all As, you're on the right track. If you answered any Bs you should probably take a few steps back to figure out if this relationship is a good fit for you. If you've found yourself checking off lots of Cs, you probably don't have a good grasp of the reality of your relationship (and it's probably not a great one). If you fall into the B or C category, go back to Chapter 3 and reread the section on "Wasting Time."

Stress-Busting Tips

Stress can be lethal to your physical health and mental health, making you look and feel like a sad sack or at times a raging lunatic. People under stress have diminished judgment and patience and have a hard time enjoying friends and family on a night out, let alone a potential mate. So don't fool yourself—no matter how much you think you have accomplished or can accomplish under stress, you are less lovable and less considerate when you're harried. While everyone experiences periods of stress, it's not a sustainable state to live in and certainly not to date in. It is essential to de-stress in order to give yourself a real chance for success in this twelve-month program. The most stressed out people are often that way by choice. They let things get to them, take work far too seriously and have a hard time letting go. If that sounds like you, you may very well already know what you need to do to pull some serenity and balance into your life but try applying even a few of the tips below. Not all circumstances can be immediately changed but you need to improve as many areas of your life as possible. If you can't at this moment, it may be a good time for a dating sabbatical.

> ## Love Notes
> *There is no good reason to stay in a relationship that's not right for you. Get the jump on the dump.*

Consult Your Ten-Year-Old Self

When you filled out your Love Résumé in Chapter 1, you answered a question about what you liked best when you were ten years old. At that age, before the pressures of puberty consumed you, you were doing some things you loved simply because they brought you joy. Look back on what brought you the most happiness when you were ten, and try to incorporate it into your adult life now. Did you bang pots and pans together much to the chagrin of your parents? Consider getting a drum set or tambourine now. Did you like to play in a pond? Get a book on marine biology. Were you always with your friends? Make friends and set play dates. Did you read? Schedule time in every day to read something you enjoy. You may get wiser about most things as you get older, but your ten-year-old self knows at least one of the best ways to reduce your stress.

Limit Your Plugged-In Time

It's a good idea to educate yourself on current events, politics, and sports, but it's important to know when to turn down the volume. Media all around you screams negativity all day. Newspapers, TV, and radio focus on car wrecks and crime. Read and listen to less disaster reporting, or choose less sensational news programs. If you feel you have to watch, you must focus on the positive. If there's a 30 percent chance of rain, that means a 70 percent chance of no rain! Turn off the BlackBerry and the Internet for at least two hours every day if you're on your own, and three hours if you are in a relationship or with a potential mate. Substitute books, music, non-sedentary activities, and face time with pleasant people, and you will feel like you are on vacation. It will reduce your work stress and your overall life stress, leaving you with more energy for dating or relating.

Exercise

As we discussed in Chapter 4, exercise is a behavioral antidepressant and a stress reducer. It tones your body and improves your health. That's a win-win-win situation. Some people find yoga to be the most calming exercise of all, because it involves meditation. Others are able to clear their minds only when running for long periods of time. For some people, playing Frisbee with their dog is the most stress-reducing exercise of all. If you find you're having a hard time getting motivated, ask one of your support team members to be a workout buddy. Even if it's just one or two mornings or evenings a week, you'll be amazed at how any situation can seem less stressful after a good sweat.

Limit Your Alcohol Intake

For some people, a glass of wine or two is a great social lubricant or a signal to relax. But even just one glass too many can cause you to do or say something you'll regret and mar your judgment about who you wish to be with and in what circumstances. Limit your drinking on dates and at all other times as well. If nothing else, you'll have more energy and probably lose a few pounds in the process.

Reduce Expectations

Reducing your expectations should apply to all areas of your life. Extend the time you give yourself (and others) for tasks. Forget multi-tasking and embrace taking care of issues and situations one at a time as they arise. Forgive your own mistakes. Schedule unscheduled time each day. And remember: your life is not a romantic comedy, you're not perfect, and your dream mate won't be either. Accept that and finding true happiness can be nearly stress-free and even over-the-top happy.

Improve Your Surroundings

Your home is your nest and it should be your little piece of heaven here on earth. If it's not, make it that way. Rearrange, paint, repair, or change as needed to make it a place you enjoy playing, meditating or praying, exercising, cooking, being loving with the man in your life, and relaxing. You want to feel welcomed and comfortable when you first walk in the door. Streamline your atmosphere. Clutter is stressful, so if you don't love or need something, give it away or throw it away, and organize everything else.

> **Love Notes**
> You can't eliminate all of the stress from your life, but you should trim the fat where you can.

Picture Yourself as You Want to Be

Your life will probably never be completely stress-free; work, family, and the push-and-pull of everyday life guarantees it. But if you go into your new dating life with a positive outlook and as little stress as possible, you'll find dating is much easier and much more enjoyable than you ever imagined. Throughout every day, practice the truth of the Einstein quote: "Your imagination is the prediction of your future." If you're feeling uninspired, look back at your Spouse Shopping List in Chapter 2. You can have that person in your life, and you will. Reflect on the goals you recorded at the end of Chapter 4. Just assume success and enjoy the feeling of being a winner. It will help you get there.

{ PART 2
LET THE SEARCH
BEGIN! }

Congratulations! The prep work for finding your dream mate is done! Give yourself a pat on the back, buy yourself dinner, or reward yourself with a piece of clothing or jewelry that makes you look and feel fabulous. Getting yourself to a place where you're truly ready to date and find your dream mate can sometimes be a painful challenge, especially when you have to take a good, hard look at yourself and face things you'd rather not. But once you're there, the real fun begins. So let the search begin!

Chapter 6

Take the Field

Myth: True love will fall from the sky.
Truth: True love could be right around the corner.

As you start searching for your soul mate, the most important thing to keep in mind is that, as much as you might want him to, the perfect guy isn't just going to fall from the sky. In bad made-for-television movies, a woman could be walking down the street and a complete stranger might approach her with love in his eyes saying, "You! You're the one for me!" But you should know that's about as likely as waking up with fresh breath and a face full of perfectly applied makeup. This is real life, not a bad movie or a romance novel. So it's time to get real about finding real love. Luckily, the keys to finding real love are pretty simple: activity, social networking (the kind you do on the computer and out in the real world), and charming assertiveness—which beats out passivity, isolation, and low energy every single time. By learning how to be charmingly assertive in every aspect of your life, you transform everything you do, every trip you take—even, or especially, if it's just to the grocery store—into an opportunity to meet the person of your dreams. Putting yourself out there—anywhere, everywhere!—is the first step.

Put Yourself Out There

The best way to meet the right man is to first meet many people. And the best way to do that is by expanding your social circle—something that's not going to happen while you're sitting alone in your living room. Realize, however, that not every guy you meet will or has to be a keeper, but there's nothing wrong with getting some practice. From now until your engagement (allowing for some sabbaticals or recess periods), you should be going out two times a week anywhere you could conceivably meet your dream mate or the person who will introduce you to him. That is twice a week every week, and three times a week if you don't have children.

If it means that you have to cut back on overtime, friend time, family time, or volunteer time, do it. Even if you don't start dating for another week or another month, this "free" time is your time and you will need to use it to prepare to meet new people and date. Maybe you'll use one evening to set up an online dating profile. Maybe you'll use another evening to attend a singles mixer. Whatever you do, make sure you dedicate two to three evenings a week to your new goal. And if you need to, get a calendar and write a heart or some other symbol on those dates so you don't get back into the habit of filling up your schedule with things you don't really want or need to do and that don't promote your marriage goal. Soon, those hearts will be followed by the names of people you're dating. Until then, they're yours, starting now.

> ### Love Notes
> When you marry, you will probably be living under the same roof, so geographical undesirability is a temporary condition.

This may seem like a lot of time out, but be sure to keep those dates. Nobody should stand you up for date night, not even yourself. You might be a little tired at first, but that's okay. Complaining about the effort involved in getting dressed, getting a sitter, and/or going out so often when you've been accustomed to a drink, TV, or book and an old robe is okay. But you still have to do it. Once you meet the man of your dreams, you're going to be going out a lot, so you might as well get used to the new schedule now.

> **Love Notes**
> *Set dates to meet dates.*
> *This is your pipeline for meeting your mate.*

Oh, the Places You'll Go

You can meet people anywhere, but being strategic about it widens your dating pool. Be more deliberate in scouting and meeting men when going to the places you already frequent, and try new places, too. Many women met their soul mates at the following places, so get out there and give it a go!

Church

If you are a church-, temple-, mosque-, or synagogue-going person, a place of worship could be a great place for you to meet the man of your dreams. But you can't just sit in the pew, expecting to meet Mr. Right. You need to get there early, help brew the coffee, or hand out bulletins. Volunteer to usher. Loiter after the service. As Benjamin Franklin said, "God helps those who help themselves." So help yourself by being proactive, even in God's house.

If you know everyone in your congregation, and know there's no one there for you, and none of your fellow congregants are introducing you to single men, then perhaps you should explore other churches. Even if you don't want to give up your group on your regular day of worship, most congregations have extracurricular activities throughout the week and many even have singles groups. Consider joining one, but be sure to get the lay of the land as quickly as possible. Virtually every religious group has a few permanent singles. Nobody is going to throw them out, but they're not shopping, either.

You could go back in ten years, and they'd still be there, and they'd still be single. That's fine, but you'll be doing yourself a favor by asking something like, "How long have you been a member of the group?" when you meet someone who piques your interest. Even church groups that aren't created for singles can be incredibly beneficial to your dating life. Networking is networking—and even married people have single friends.

LOVE STORIES: ISOBEL

Isobel was a devoted Christian whose church of choice was a small neighborhood congregation that perfectly suited her spiritual needs but seemed like too small of a pond for fishing. She went to the bigger churches' singles groups regularly but had had no luck meeting a man who interested her. One night, having nothing going on and wanting to check off that third night out, Isobel decided to attend the singles group at her home church. Everyone said it was a flop and a waste of time. But she reasoned that no matter how pathetic it was as a meeting place, it beat staying home.

As predicted, attendance was small. There were three people including Isobel. But against all odds, of the two men, one, a man named Chuck, was very interesting to her. The diminutive group provided an opportunity to talk with Chuck longer than she would have in a larger gathering and to demonstrate her graciousness in including both men in conversation, letting Chuck know she was interested without offending the other man. Chuck asked Isobel out that night and the rest is history. They are happily dating and attending their smaller church every Sunday.

Bars

Bars sometimes get a bad rap, but they can be great places to meet single men. You just have to go to the right bar at the right time, and have the right attitude and look when you do. Going to a bar near a college campus on Friday night if you're a forty-year-old woman would be an example of the wrong bar at the wrong time, and virtually any accessory will be wrong and so will your jeans. But if you visit a bar near the financial district of your city at 6 P.M. on a Thursday or Friday and happen to be sitting alone with a drink and a good book about politics or a copy of *The New Yorker*, you're probably on the right track.

When you find the bar or bars that are right for you, and you're ready to go alone, take along a book or a project so you don't look desperate and be sure to look up a lot and smile so you don't look too busy. If you're reading on your PDA or phone, someone might worry about interrupting a text or phone conversation and not want to approach. Checking your watch is a good touch, too; this signals you might be meeting someone so if a man is interested in meeting you, he'd better hop on it because your time is limited. But no matter what you do, remember to always convey an air of interesting and approachable. If the idea of going to a bar alone worries you, start out by trying lunch at a bar. It's generally something only men do, and since this is what you're looking for, that's a great place to start.

Wine Tastings

If you're a person who appreciates fine wine and food, or if the bar scene isn't for you, check out a wine tasting. Most liquor stores or vineyards offer free, regular tastings, hoping you'll buy the wines being sampled. Unlike bars, which can often make people feel either secluded or pressured into talking, wine tastings offer a great environment for starting a conversation with something other than, "So, do you come here often?"

Gallery Openings

You don't have to know a lot, or anything, about art to successfully meet people at a gallery opening. Sure, you might not attract the artist with your confession about not knowing the difference between abstract expressionism and impressionist paintings, but asking a question of a fellow gallery patron is a great way to start a very natural conversation. Gallery openings usually have refreshments, too, so you have something to do with your hands as well as a spot to stand where most people will eventually come to you.

Networking Events

Yes, people go to networking events to find clients, potential employers, or people who can help them in any given industry. But men in particular have been known to use networking events like singles mixers if the opportunity is there, and you should, too! Not only will you have a room full of people who are there to talk, many will be successful at what they do. You might not meet Mr. Right at the Chamber of Commerce networking event, but his business partner might want to introduce you to him at the next one.

Singles Events

Singles events and single-parent mixers can be great places to meet your mate, but they can also be incredibly deceiving. Like anything else you try, check out the numbers. If they're small, or the female-to-male ratio is way out of proportion, look elsewhere. If you find a single-parent mixer that you like, and have specific requirements for your mate's children (say, you only want to date someone whose children are grown and out of the house), then make sure those are the kinds of questions you're asking up front. If you have children of your own, even if they drive you up a wall, be very positive about them. You can deal with reality later and hopefully have dealt better with your children.

Join the Club

For just about every interest, there is a club or class out there—coffee, rock climbing, running, cycling, boxing, computer skills, investing, bowling, beer brewing—the list goes on. Identify what it is you like to do, match it with where the men go, and meet up with them on a regular basis. To help you out, choose classes that have opposite sex appeal. Take classes on home or car repair, how to start your own business, architecture, computers, real estate, comedy, film, finance, golf, politics, world affairs, or fly fishing. Or choose some classes just for your own interests. You probably won't meet the man of your dreams in a sewing circle, but you might meet his sister there. That's why it's important to always be positively assertive, unharried, dressed for meeting her brother in case he's the one giving her a ride home, and in a good mood, wherever you are. Your classmate won't want to set you up with her brother or best male friend if you're crabby and depressed about the lack of men in your life, or look like you put so little effort into attracting men that you might frighten some. Do what you enjoy, but don't limit yourself only to activities you know you do well. Expanding your interests is good for your mind. This doesn't mean you need to take up hunting if you want a rugged, outdoorsy man, but you might decide to go camping with friends (and their friends!), or take canoeing or rock climbing lessons.

LOVE STORIES: JAMINA

Jamina was a very attractive attorney who had invested her time and energy into her career with little to no thought about marriage. Her life as a single was good with many friends but she was ready to move into the next phase and was seriously considering marriage as her next goal. The year Jamina graduated from my class the students organized an ongoing social group that met at a restaurant near Emory and gave an open invitation to each new class to join. Jamina joined the group and was still there when the next new class graduated and joined the group.

One evening about a year later, Fritz, a Germanic looking, stay-at-home writer and father of three, who kept lots of time open for play and non-work related projects, walked in the door. He was not Jamina's type. She had planned on a personality that was similar to her own, but the chemistry was there from the start. Jamina and Fritz kept talking long after the party was over and until the restaurant closed. They started dating and four months later they married.

While getting married that quickly can be a negative, I do believe soul mates know each other when they meet and so-called rules cease to apply. Jamina and Fritz met ten years ago and happily re-visited the class to share their love story.

Anywhere

You can meet someone anywhere, as long as you have the right attitude. If you're somebody who is open, tends to chat—not just to men but to all of the people around you—you're making yourself easy to befriend. You, too, can be one of those women who starts conversations with available men (just make certain that he is taking over the initiative at some point).

People often say they have game faces to get themselves pumped up for parties or dates to increase their level of confidence. If your game face means you're outgoing, friendly, and charming, wear it all the time, as long as you're in safe territory. You can meet people at even the most unexpected places if you're willing to strike up a conversation with anybody. You will expand your social circle and seem more approachable to the shy but possibly marriage-ready man across the room.

Love Notes

Be an equal-opportunity chatter.

As you start putting yourself out there looking for that perfect guy, keep in mind that you are your own best resource when it comes to meeting new people. You know the kinds of places you're comfortable going and what you like doing. But it's important to seek out and ask for help, too. Be open to more opportunities to expand your dating pool.

Your Best Places

We all get stuck in ruts. Sometimes we even forget the things we like to do or great suggestions we've heard. So put it in print. Get your pen and identify the types of places you enjoy and activities you love to do, then schedule the time to actually do these things. And don't be afraid to put yourself out there and add on new experiences. Sometimes even the strangest things work; there was one woman who did all her nursing school homework in a comfortable chair outside a men's room at the med school. She eventually met and married the doctor of her choice.

> ### Love Notes
> *Put on a happy face. It's the most attractive accessory you can wear. Your smile and happiness level are your best advertisement.*

Where to Go List

Take a few minutes to write down all of the places you'd like to go or think you could go to meet new people, whether they're dates or people who could introduce you to potential dates.

_____

_____

_____

_____

_____

_____

Think about what you can enjoy in each one of those places, even if you might not frequent them for any other reason. The more you enjoy yourself when you're out, the more someone will want to enjoy being out (or at home) with you.

Before You Go

Like it or not, many possible dates will assess you and decide whether or not to approach you often based solely on how you look. So it's important that you're not just concerned about date-dressing, but that you're doing attract-a-date dressing. Granted, everyone wants to be loved for themselves, and the ultimate goal of a good marriage is unconditional love. But in order to get it, you need to attract enough potential mates in the first place.

Clean Out Your Closet

When you're shopping for a mate, dating, and even once you're married, you always want to look your best (fallback being you are willing to look in the mirror). Because when you look your best, you usually feel your best, which benefits you and everyone around you, whether you're at a gallery opening or making a quick run to the grocery store at 9 P.M. If you clean up really well, do it all the time, starting right now. If not, you know that the moment you're running around in baggy sweatpants with three-day hair could be the moment you pass by the man of your dreams in the dairy aisle. You don't need to look like you spend every minute in front of a mirror, but when you feel frumpy, you act differently—you might not make eye contact, smile or chat up the nice-looking man at the fruit stand.

As you're putting things on your social calendar, write "Closet" on an upcoming day or night. Take that time to go through your wardrobe and get rid of every piece of clothing that doesn't help you feel good about yourself. Sell or give away those clothes and buy a few pieces that make you feel great! If you need to, seek professional advice on cuts and colors. You only need a few outfits beyond your work and play clothes, and you can always rotate really great pieces. If you have a fantastic first-date outfit, that should always be your first-date outfit. Switch things up a bit for the second and third. By the time you're seriously dating someone, he's not going to notice or care that you mix and match the same five or six pieces, as long as they're always clean and fresh.

Look Fresh-Faced

Even if you're not a person who wears a lot of makeup, you should have one go-to product. Whether it's a shade of lipstick that lights up your entire face, or a luxurious mascara that makes you feel like you have beautiful eyes, make an effort to make yourself up just a little. If you don't wear any makeup at all, it should only be because you take fantastic care of your skin and your features don't require it. Makeup shouldn't make you look like a clown, and it shouldn't remain on his clothes if you snuggle, but it does accentuate the positive and reduce the negative. Done well, it is like an invisible arrow directing gazes to the feature of your choice and away from your least favorite. If you're lost when it comes to cosmetics, consider visiting a pro or your best-looking, noncompetitive friend for a free consultation on quick and easy ways to make you feel like a million bucks with just a few swipes every morning and evening.

How-to-Behave-When-You-Get-There Rules

Getting there is half the battle. The other half is knowing how to act once you get there. It's a cliché, but beauty really is only skin deep. Appearance is just the beginning of what men find attractive in a potential partner. You need to have brains *and* a personality. Now that you're taking the field, you can't go to all these wonderful places ready to meet people, then just stand there like a well-dressed stone. Most women pay attention to their looks when they go out, but not their personality. And it's personality that wins every time.

> ## Love Notes
> *Don't just look fabulous.*
> *Be fabulous.*

Pretend You're the Greeter

When you get to an event, take it upon yourself to meet as many people as you can, by taking on the unofficial role of host or hostess. You not only automatically meet more people, you make everyone else in the room more comfortable and make yourself incredibly approachable. Your future dream mate might not be at this particular event, but you may impress enough people to get invited to another event where you will meet him.

LOVE STORIES: KATE

Kate was a super strong, fifty-something executive who was very intimidating with her designer business suits and her firm handshakes. She exuded authority and clout and was very off-putting to a lot of men she met. After taking my class, she took on the role of advocate and recommended the class to her friends and every single in her company, as an esteem-building technique that would be useful for any single. She set up a virtual soapbox on the corner. No longer coming across as a daunting CEO, she was showing herself as an approachable single who just wanted to help others in the same boat. She flipped her whole persona by seeming more like a nurturer than a drill captain.

One of the men skipped the class and just started dating her.

Set a Goal

Before you go somewhere, set a number of people that you promise yourself you'll meet before you leave—whether it's three, five, or ten—and do not leave until you've met your self-imposed quota. They might not all be potential mates, but whenever you meet someone new you improve your people skills and your social circle. Having a larger network, personally and professionally, can only improve your chances of meeting the man of your dreams.

Be Purposeful

Scan the room. Decide which table or which group of people is most appealing at a party before you join them. Don't just wander aimlessly from wall to wall, hoping somebody will seek you out. Look for the most interesting people, the most animated conversations, the most alluring gatherings, and head in that direction. But remember that auditions aren't meant to last forever. Even if you are interested in a man, after ten to fifteen minutes, it's time to meet someone else. Just let him know by complimenting him or through your avid interest that you'd like to hear from him again!

Be Friendly

If you're bold enough to head to a club where everyone's dancing, it won't do you any good to hug the wall. Be approachable, happy, and stay on the move. Or, dance alone for optimal visibility! Chances are good you'll be approached because you look approachable. Dancing is an exercise that increases endorphins, and makes you feel good. And when you feel good, you look good. Whether you're a good dancer or as awkward as all get-out, the point is to have fun. Your friendliness and willingness to enjoy talking or dancing with many different people is infinitely better than passively waiting for someone else to bring you to life.

Go Solo

It's better to go out on your own than with someone, because you're more approachable solo. When a man walks up to a group of women, he faces the whole "cut from the herd" issue. Someone's feelings could get hurt, and no woman worth her salt would want her friends offended. Also, if you tell a guy to "get lost," his rejection has an audience. If you must travel in a pack, break out often to saunter slowly around the room with confidence and smiles.

Get Some Help

Just because you're single doesn't mean you have to go it alone. And it doesn't mean that you *are* alone either. Don't be afraid to turn to your family, friends, or even a professional matchmaker to help you out on your search for love. You may be surprised at how helpful these people can be!

Get Some Help from Your Friends

By now, the friends you surround yourself with should all be very supportive of your quest to find and keep your dream mate, so be sure to communicate to all of them that you're seriously looking for a keeper this time. Turn your friends and family into matchmakers (as long as you trust their taste). Let them know you'll be appreciative of anything they send your way, and that you will not fault them in any way whatsoever if something doesn't work out. Promise (and keep to the promise) that even if you and your blind date can barely stand each other for a couple of hours, the only feedback they'll hear is praise for their effort in helping you reach your goal. Thus there is no downside for them, which will keep them trying. As they learn what does and does not work for you—and you're not making them feel bad for a match that didn't quite fit—they can be more deliberate about their selections. But just because you've promised not to criticize doesn't mean that you can't politely guide them. Sometimes people will slap two friends together only because they're both single. Ask why they think the two of you would work or simply share your Spouse Shopping List with them.

Acting as a matchmaker yourself can also work to your advantage. If you're the one who's always setting up your friends, they're going to want to repay the favor. If somebody is really great, just maybe not so great for you, think about who else might like him. The favor will most likely be returned someday because you have two people invested in helping you.

Family

Occasionally, family members are good at setting people up. When you're young, you'd never want to date someone your mother likes, but your mother or child could meet someone perfect for you while riding on a plane or at a business cocktail party. Your mom might embarrass you with the old, "Would you like to meet my daughter" routine, but if she's talking to a man who's really interested in meeting someone, he'll find it charming. It will also prove that you have a good relationship with your mother, which is a plus.

> ### Love Notes
> It's okay to date someone your mom likes. And even better if your kids like him, too. But don't introduce him until you have labeled him "potential keeper."

Children on the lookout are also very charming. If they're young children trying to set you up, it shows they're pretty well adjusted to whatever changes have occurred in your family and that they are mature enough to truly want you to be happy. If they're older and have turned out well, it's a great reflection on you.

Matchmakers

If you're going to use a matchmaking service, make sure you do your homework before you sign up. The prices can be insane and the description of the pool of people they have available may be less than scrupulously accurate. You want your matchmaker to be the right match, too! Sometimes a matchmaker will take you in, even if he or she doesn't have any matches for you. You're trying to make your dating pool as large as possible, so if someone or something is going to narrow it, that may not be the right move. If you do find a person or service with a big pool, then get specific about what you want in a dream mate—after all, you're paying them to shop for your mate and meet your description as closely as possible. After you meet with a matchmaker, ask "What type of person do you see me being matched with?" and be prepared to come back with your Spouse Shopping List items and tell him or her, "These are the things that are important to me." Every time a matchmaker sets you up, make sure that person matches your top three items. But also listen to your matchmaker; the best of the best will have good ideas about whom you should be with. Don't be afraid to ask questions like, "Why do you think we would be a good match?" and "What are some of the things we have in common?"

Online Dating Sites

More and more people are meeting through online dating sites. This once-taboo way to meet a mate is now commonplace for daters of all ages. Now that people do just about everything through the Internet, meeting people on an online dating site just doesn't seem so strange. And it shouldn't—a well-written profile can get the big, important things out there right away (age, religion, children, what kind of relationship you want) while leaving just enough mystery to be intriguing. And please don't give out more personal information than is safe or more than you are getting back in return. But, buyer beware: while some sites might be good for someone looking for a quick hookup, this is not you. You want a serious relationship, so make sure you're using serious sites.

One clue is that men who are more committed to finding spouses are willing to pay to use a service that's not cluttered with fake profiles and people looking for a quick hookup. Another clue is whether or not they've chosen a site that requires a lengthy questionnaire for matching. If a man plans on sticking with the woman he finds, he's more than a little interested in having compatible personalities. Try one or try a few of the plethora of dating sites, and treat them the way you would any other way to meet people: be open, courteous, and kind, but if someone contacts you and it doesn't feel right, it probably isn't. If a guy is giving you the creeps, act on your instinct and disconnect from him immediately. And if the Internet gives you the creeps, there are still plenty of ways to meet people out in the real world.

LOVE STORIES: MILLIE

When it came to dating, Millie's number-one rule was try absolutely everything for longer than she thought she could stand it. She believed that no matter how discouraging a place may have been at first, wherever she was could be the place she'd meet her mate and this held true when it came to dating online. In fact, Millie may have had the longest standing eHarmony account to date. She definitely deleted more men than most women ever meet, and dated more than most deleted. But after two-and-a-half years online, she finally connected with her dream guy. Jacob met every criteria on her spouse shopping list and then some. He was crazy about her and they obviously fit together beautifully. Her family and friends were thrilled. Millie and Jacob dated for two years before their recent marriage, which felt right for them. They share online dating horror stories with laughter, but more importantly, their focus is on achieving marital bliss, which sounds like a beautiful goal no matter how you look at it.

Wherever You Go, There You Are

No matter where you go, or how you do it, it's still your attitude that is going to help you play the field. Remember to be charmingly assertive wherever you are, at any time, because every moment is an opportunity. Change up your routine, walk a different way to work, offer to share your umbrella, borrow a dog and go to the park, or "accidentally" cut in front of an attractive man at the coffee shop then apologize profusely. You never know when you'll meet your dream mate, so from this point on, you should always be ready for him.

Chapter 7

The Simple Rules of Dating

Myth: Dating is something you have to slog through to get your man.

Truth: If you are doing this right, you feel great, are enjoying yourself, and know that dating is not a funeral. It is an opportunity.

Do you remember a time when dating was fun and exciting, when every date was a new possibility? Unfortunately, as time goes on, dating often becomes intimidating or dreadful or both. But it doesn't have to be. In fact, it shouldn't be at all! When you date, you need to keep your heart wide open. It's okay to enjoy dating with the heart of a sixteen-year-old, as long as you also keep the head of an adult who has experience and wisdom and knows what she wants out of the rest of her life. And if you've done all of the work in this book up to this point, you're in a great place to enjoy dating because you recognize it's a step in the right direction toward meeting and marrying your dream mate. Still, whether you're new to dating, or looking for a second or third marriage, chances are good that your dating style could use an update. That's where the Simple Rules of Dating—and a few reminders on some dating dos and don'ts—come into play.

Simple Rules for Dating

There are all kinds of books, websites, and programs that claim to have *the* rules for dating, but be careful to take these sources with a grain of salt. After all, any book that tells you to play games or to pretend to be different from who you are, for example, may not be the best choice to help you reach your goal of marriage. So make sure that any dating rules that you follow make sense for you—and not just dating, but for the rest of your life as well. Think about it: if you wouldn't play mind games with your best friends or family members to get what you want, why on earth would you want to play mind games with someone you hope will someday become part of your family? You wouldn't and you shouldn't. Game playing is not only exhausting, it keeps you in a constant state of pretense and is unsustainable. You want to date with credibility. When you get past the dating and courting stage, you should still be recognizable. If your dating life consists of game playing, you simply won't be credible *or* recognizable. You might not even be attractive to your mate anymore.

> **Love Notes**
> The better you look, the better you'll feel, and vice versa. Make an effort to look good and feel good every day.

You should also keep in mind that dating rules are never one-size-fits-all. Any set of dating rules, these or any others, will not fit everyone all the time. So use these rules as a guide. Try on a rule and see if it fits. If it doesn't, it might not be a rule for you, and that's okay. Feel free to adjust the rules to fit your lifestyle and sensibilities. After all, what's important is that you're doing what works for you.

Men Have to Want to Meet You in Order to Date You

Yes, it's what inside that matters most, but that doesn't mean that how you present yourself on the outside doesn't matter at all—especially when we're dealing with men, who are very visual creatures. Like it or not, many possible dates will assess you and decide whether or not to approach you often based solely on how you look or on how they see you act. It doesn't mean you need to look like a supermodel, but you do need to look as though you're on top of your game, and you need to show that you've made some effort. This signifies you want to attract—it's a mating signal. So remember that you're not just date-dressing—you are attract-a-date dressing. After all, everywhere you go, you could meet him, so make sure you're always prepared.

Turnoffs for Men

Keep in mind that not all men are turned off by all of these things—and, in some cases, some of them may qualify as nitpicking. But if you're a woman who's guilty of even one of these "dating sins," it doesn't hurt to take the time to get ahead of the game.

1. Terminal cuteness
2. Chattering
3. Descriptions of former lovers
4. Chronic lateness
5. Wearing too much makeup
6. Being too materialistic
7. Being incapable of stating what she needs and wants without an emotional meltdown
8. Truly helpless women
9. Male bashers
10. Non-reciprocators

Pay special attention to number eight, and if you feel that describes you, it's time for a change in priorities. Men don't want clinging vines. In today's world, they have enough to take care of without the additional burden of a helpless woman who can't balance the checkbook, meet new people, or be a helpmate instead of a helpless mate. They generally want a wife who helps them face life.

Be Fabulous (Don't Just Look Fabulous)

Appearance is just the beginning of what both sexes find attractive in a potential partner. So, be prepared with topics of conversation. Be complimentary, friendly, kind, polite, and culturally literate. Learn how to approach and be approached graciously, issue invitations, make suggestions for outings, and be expressively appreciative. If you don't think you're charming, take the time to reread Chapter 4. Having the right attitude really does make all the difference in the world of dating—and in life.

Ten Turn-Ons for Men

This list is compiled from thousands of men in my classes and practice through the years. These are their favorite qualities about women. Notice that many of them describe behaviors.

1. Physical affection (usually including public displays of affection)
2. A sense of humor
3. Intelligence
4. Commitment to a career or other interest
5. Well-cared-for body
6. Generosity
7. Ability to listen without telling him what to do, and ability to tell him what she wants but not how to do it
8. Honesty, especially in finances
9. Common values
10. Low level of drama

Contrary to popular belief, most men aren't looking for perfect bodies and people pleasers. Like women, men want to someone to talk to, to listen to them, to trust and to love.

Be Yourself

This doesn't mean you should belch at the dinner table or tell your entire life story on the first date. In fact, you should always be on your best behavior when you're dating, especially in the early stages. But make sure it's really *your* best behavior and that you're not trying to emulate something or someone you think your date will like better. By doing that, you're ultimately setting yourself up for failure, and fear will eventually get the best of you. One of a dater's biggest fears is worrying that a man will leave once he gets to know the real woman. If you're the real you from the get-go, you have nothing to worry about. The less you pretend, the more relaxed you'll be, and there's nothing more attractive than appearing, and actually *being*, relaxed on a date.

> **Love Notes**
> Let a date get to know the real you from the start. Just be sure to start with the most positive possible version of you.

Flirt Like Crazy!

In dating, flirting is mandatory! Some people are natural flirts, but it's a skill that absolutely anyone can learn. All you have to do is give the following a try:

- **Smile.** This is a crucial first step to flirting. I encourage my students to learn by practicing on small animals and furniture. Add people you know, then graduate to strangers in safe territory.
- **Make eye contact.** If you don't hold eye contact for at least four seconds, he will interpret it as rejection, not come-hither.

After you break eye contact, look back again and smile. If you look approachable and he is mobile, if he wants to meet you, he will.

- **Stand up straight.** By doing so you'll appear more confident, and you'll feel more confident—which will make flirting much easier. I promise.
- **Hold something back.** This doesn't mean you have to keep all of your cards close, but let him pull out something interesting about you. Once he does, he'll want to work harder to find out more.
- **Be playful.** Watching someone who is not at all playful try to flirt can be painful. You don't need to act like a child, a damsel in distress (remember, men often don't care for helpless women), or a professional vamp or tramp, but if there's one game you should play when dating, it is being playful. It's fun, makes you seem like fun, and is the fast road to seeming cute.

These tips aren't about deception, they're about presentation and intrigue. In the beginning, getting to know someone is part of the fun, so let him do a little bit of the work to get there. Chances are he wants to.

Talk to Strangers

Strangers get a bad rap, but in most cases, strangers are nice people—and you're not going to meet your dream mate if you don't talk to some of them. But guess what? Once you start talking to someone, he's not a stranger anymore. If you're uncomfortable talking to strangers, keep a list of conversation starters like the following and try them out daily:

- "You look terrific in that!" Say it to anyone wearing anything—even if they're in tatters, they'll find it funny.
- "I know you from somewhere." People always like to figure out how they might know someone. (Later you can admit to your not-so-subtle ruse.)
- "Can you tell me what the Dow is today?" This will only work if they're reading the *Wall Street Journal* or appear to be checking stocks digitally, but for that crowd, it will work.
- "I can recommend a great book." This, of course, is best used in a bookstore.
- "I couldn't help overhearing your conversation." This is useful if you'd like to butt in.
- "What kind of dog, car, computer, etc., is that?" Showing interest in another person's choices is always good.
- "I'm newly single and am trying out pickup lines. Could you tell me what works best with you?"

These are just suggestions. If something feels awkward, don't say it. Say what feels comfortable to you, even if it's just "I'm really uncomfortable talking to strangers, but . . . "

Love Notes
The bigger your net, the more potential partners you'll have to choose from.

Be an Effective Browser

In the next chapter, we'll discuss being a smart shopper—a woman who has made her list before she starts, knows what fits her and what doesn't, and won't be buying if the emotional price is too high or if a guy is not what she is looking for. But before you shop, you should browse. Often women report feeling overwhelmed when faced with a room full of strangers, or they complain about getting stuck in a corner with the first person who speaks to them. Because they feel out of control in new social situations, they let valuable opportunities for meeting potential dream mates slip away. You need to take control of your own social experiences. Start small and work your way up; scan the room, choose three to ten people to meet, and then initiate conversations. Auditions aren't meant to last forever. Even if you are interested, after ten minutes it's time to meet someone else—after letting him know you'd like to hear from him again, of course!

Let Him Get to Know You First

Successful daters act desirable, not desperate. So before you start spilling all the dark secrets and sad stories of your difficult past, let your potential mate find out about the intriguing you in the present. Sometimes women can give up too much information too early in a relationship, and you'll find very few women who got married because they needed a daddy, wanted a stepparent for their kids, couldn't manage their lives, or were afraid to be alone. A healthy mate will be attracted to responsibility, self-respect, the ability to nurture, and the ability to be a friend.

> **Love Notes**
> *No one is perfect, and no one expects you to be perfect.*

LOVE STORIES: TANYA

Tanya was overweight, but beautiful with a great personality. After really soaking in a class segment about identifying and promoting your strong points and holding off revealing your flaws until after a few dates, Tanya had come up with a plan. She would focus her online dating profile on her personality and pretty face and leave blank the "body type" check boxes. "When they meet me, they'll be initially surprised," she said, "but I think I can win someone over with my personality."

Tanya never got a chance to try out her new strategy because, released from her "no one will date me because I'm overweight, so why try" attitude, she instantly became more self-confident. She asked out the quiet accountant named Rudy sitting next to her, and within a year, they were engaged and four years later are still happily married.

> ## Love Notes
> *Your man has to feel you know him in order to feel your love.*

Sniff Out Boundaries Early On

One thing that's evident about relationships is that each partner quickly learns how far they can toe the line, but when you first start to date someone, you need to pay close attention to where those boundaries lie. For example, some dating books recommend that when a woman goes into a man's house for the first time, she should do something to advertise her domestic skills, like cleaning, tidying, or cooking. Some men have said that would be a huge turnoff and they each have their different reasons: it's intrusive, it's rude, it's controlling, it's messing with your stuff, etc. And there are some men who've said they would love it. But no matter the topic, every man knows what he wants, and one way or the other, he'll let you know right up front. Be sensitive to your date's boundaries from the get-go. It will make everything going forward a lot more pleasant and respectful for both of you.

Listen

If you are sticking to the schedule so far, you've already been practicing good listening skills, so that by the time you do take the field,
listening on a date shouldn't be a problem. In fact, go back and retake
the "Are You a Good Listener?" quiz in Chapter 3. You should pass
with flying colors! Apply those skills to your dates as well as every single interaction in your daily life. It will make everyone around you—
from the clerk at the grocery store to your future spouse—feel cared
for and respected. As a bonus, listening carefully will also make your
job easier. Contrary to popular belief, understanding men really isn't
that much of a mystery. They can be ambivalent and send conflicting
signals, but if you give them the opportunity, they'll tell you what it is
they really want.

Have Fun

This one should be a given, but for most women, actually having
fun is the hardest part of dating. Approach each date as something
with exciting potential—be it for friendship, love, marriage, a good
laugh down the line, etc.—and you'll have fun. Even if you have a
bad date, it could still be a nice dinner or a great story. On the other
hand, if you go into each date with fear, negativity, and little effort,
then not only will you not enjoy yourself, you could be turning off
a man who could have been "the one." And isn't finding "the one"
why you're here? If you're worried about having fun while you date,
try asking him to plan dates that will be fun for you and then make
an effort to plan some yourself. Do you like board games? Make a
night of Scrabble, good food, and great company. Do you like walking around the city? Pick a series of bars and restaurants and stop
into each one for a small plate. And wherever you go, when you get
there, relax! If one date doesn't work out, at least you have a little
more practice under your belt. Even better, you're one date closer to
finding your dream mate!

LOVE STORIES: DONNA

After two dates, Donna decided she just wasn't that into Gerald. But they shared a love for bluegrass music. So, even after she let him know she no longer wanted to date, they decided they would still see bluegrass shows together. One Wednesday afternoon, Gerald called with a last-minute invite to a show at a bar near Donna's office. She decided to go, and it's a good thing she did! She met the man who would later become her husband at that show. A few weeks later, Gerald met someone he began dating, too. They don't keep in touch anymore, but Donna still credits Gerald with helping her meet her husband.

Dating DON'Ts and DOs

It's now time to take a look at our pretty hefty list of dating DOs and DON'Ts. Some of them are just basic common sense; others might surprise you. They range from rules to apply at your very first interaction to rules that will apply in committed relationships. Some are self-explanatory; others need a little more explanation. As with the rest of the rules in this chapter, they might not all be a perfect fit for you. Find the ones that work for you, and go with them. You'll notice that the Dos are the end, because like with a date, you should never end on a negative note. Bookmark these DON'Ts and DOs and refer to them often.

Dating DON'Ts

Dating should be more about the positive than the negative, but there are still some things any smart dater should avoid. Keep these don'ts in the back of your mind to avoid some of the most common dating mistakes.

- **Don't nag, complain, get angry, swear, or drink too much on the first date, and little if any on future dates.** If that's his best behavior, you don't want to see his worst. And if he doesn't care enough to be on his best behavior on a first date, you don't want to date him anyway!

- **Understand that if the other person is less-than-wonderful, they still might be a great mate.** They might care, they might be nervous, they might not have had a trillion dating experiences. It's easy to be smooth and unflappable when you aren't invested, and you know you're not going beyond a few dates.

- **Don't go where one person knows everyone, and the other knows no one.** This could be uncomfortable for the person who doesn't know a soul. They might feel stared at and judged—and they might be stared at and judged. They also might feel your choice is a power play. Preferably, keep it more or less equal and on mutual or new turf for the first time.

- **Don't talk too much about work on any date, even if you love your job.** At least pretend you have balance in your life at the beginning. If you're going to accomplish a good marriage in the future, you'll need to develop it anyway.

- **Don't talk about your ex.** There's a matchmaking group in New York called Godmothers. They asked their clients what was the worst thing that happens on a first date. Almost everyone said the same thing: hearing about the ex. It's boring. It also communicates that you're still carrying baggage. And your date will assume quite correctly that where you're going to dump that baggage is on him.

- **Don't name-call.** As we've previously discussed, character assassination is not foreplay. Your date wants to be treated like a person, not immediately and verbally lumped into the "jerk" category with all of your exes and Charles Manson. If he upsets you, let him know with words—preferably ones that imply you have faith he could change—but never names.

- **Don't interrupt.** You'll never know how he would have finished his sentence, and if you always think you do, you're delusional. Interrupting is rude, even if you think it conveys your similar thinking. All it really conveys is your poor ability to listen. Trust me, he'll be far more impressed with your listening skills than your overly quick come-back.

- **Don't get involved with people with untreated chronic mental illness.** This does not mean people who have solved problems. Given a choice, you're better off with someone who's had problems and successfully dealt with adversity. Nobody gets out of life without having a few problems. You are looking for somebody to marry who is good at whatever life throws at him, not someone to adopt.

- **Don't get involved with somebody whose ability to care just isn't there.** It can be great to be the initiator, the positive one, the enthusiastic one in a relationship. No relationship is precisely 50/50. But if it gets past 65 percent on your part, then you need to reassess. Hold back, do a little less, speak up a little more, and say, "Would you do this for me?" Ask for more things to find out if you can be on the receiving end and aren't blocking him from giving. Being a giver is a great thing to be, but too many givers believe the reward is coming without any verification. Ask yourself if you are satisfied with your mate's willingness to give as well as to take. Ask him if he is satisfied with your willingness to give as well as to take. A sense of fairness in the relationship is based on this balance and understanding.

- **Don't be rigid about rules, behaviors, or schedules.** Flexibility is a wonderful, important attribute to bring to a relationship. People who are extremely inflexible are guaranteed to be problems later on. Someone very inflexible very early in a relationship can be downright tyrannical as the years roll on.

- **Don't accept an overwhelming number of idiosyncratic behaviors.** At best, he will wear you out. At worst, you'll need to commit him.

- **Don't let assertiveness turn into aggression.** Assertiveness means, "I know what I want and I attempt to get it." Aggression is when you demand, insist, bully, manipulate, and will not settle for anything other than your way.

- **Don't get so stressed out that you make bad decisions.** Part of your task, being in training for getting married, is to continually reduce your own stress levels. (See Chapter 5.)
- **Don't be a doormat.** If you are—or have ever been accused of being a doormat—one way to overcome it is that you enter talking. Doormats often wait and see if it's okay for them to come into the conversation, and sometimes they link up with very expressive, directive people who don't let them into the conversation. An expressive thinks everybody's an expressive, so they assume you will say, "Hush, now I have something to say." You may need to have a speech ready. "Before I sit down, I want to tell you all a story. And I'm going to start talking first or I'll never get it out."
- **Don't automatically withdraw from the man who seems clinging.** If you're irritated by your pursuer, or irritated by his wanting more from you, then try stepping forward and giving more as a test. Sometimes they don't seem as clinging. What they seem is satisfied.
- **Don't stay with someone who just wants to boss you around.** Let them find another victim.
- **Don't be dazzled by anybody who is so sexy, good-looking, brilliant, powerful, successful, or from such a good family that he thinks you owe him.** Parasites come in all forms.
- **Don't expect everything to show up right away.** Some men simply don't show warmth, a sense of humor, or the best side of themselves until you've gone out—and then gone out again, and maybe again. If it's really horrible, don't give him a second chance. But if he is not horrible, but just okay, give him another try and yourself an opportunity.

- **Don't travel in herds.** It's much easier to approach someone who's alone. That doesn't mean you should go everywhere by yourself, but get a drink by yourself, walk slowly to the bathroom by yourself, and go outside to take a call by yourself. By going everywhere with your pack, you put a guy in the position of having to cut you from it. Only the bravest will approach you, because if you reject him, he'll have an audience.

- **Don't overly emphasize physical attractiveness, educational level, income, age, profession, home, dress, and car.** Emphasize sexual and emotional satisfaction, intelligence, shared interests, warmth, sense of humor, communication skills, and temperament. When you do this, you decrease your competition because you aren't going for the externals that attract the majority of people. In addition, you have a better possibility of a really good marriage because you're focusing on what *feels* good, not just what *looks* good.

- **Don't succumb to chronic fighting.** Fighting happens, but when it happens it should be to find a resolution. For some, fighting is a turn on. You yell, you scream, you throw a few things. Then you cry, you make up, and you make love. If that matches your idea of good, then great. If it doesn't match, don't participate. Stop the blame game. Skip the recriminations and go straight to this phrase: "What shall we do about this now?"

Now that you've done some behavioral de-cluttering to eliminate your largest relationship sins, it's time to develop new habits of relating that will work for you in finding and keeping your dream mate.

Dating DOs

These Dos are just suggestions for making dating better. Even if you don't follow them exactly, follow them in spirit. They're positive, fun, communicative, and respectful.

- **Do plan the first date to include an event, such as a movie, museum, concert, or walk, along with talk time.** Don't just sit and bare souls all evening. Or if that is what you want to do, only agree to a drink or coffee so that if you don't particularly like his soul, you have an easy out.
- **Do practice seeing the other person's perspective.** You might not always see eye to eye, but you can at least do your best to understand where your date or mate is coming from. Identical thinking is not necessary, but mutual respect is.
- **Do bring out the best in other people; it automatically makes you seem charming.** If you bring out the worst in people, why in the world would anyone want to get involved with you? Do your best to see the best in others, and do what you can to bring it out in them.
- **Do acquire a multitude of subjects you're able to talk about.** Women who talk about their work all the time are no more interesting than men who talk about their work all the time.
- **Do compliment people.** Make an effort to express every compliment that you think about someone. The most impressive person I ever worked with never spoke negatively about anyone, even when I knew there was plenty that could have been said. It's a great character trait.
- **Do treat your lover as well as you treat your friends.** We are capable of being nicer to strangers than we are to the man we're with, which doesn't make a lot of sense. Be courteous to everyone—but especially to the man you might love.
- **Do one thing every day to move you toward your goal.** This helps break procrastination. For example, write down the name

of someone whom you'd call and say, "I'm interested in serious commitment. I'm looking for someone I might date. Do you know anybody?" You could also start a dating profile online, attend a singles mixer, or simply change up your route so you run into new people.

- **Do get out of your house and go where there is a chance of meeting your dream mate three times a week.** You aren't going to find your dream mate at home. If you were, you'd already be happily married and you wouldn't be reading this book.
- **Do know what you want to change about your past relationships so that you are not doing the same things in new ones. There is always some room for improvement.** Repeating the same behaviors over and over again and expecting a different outcome? We all know what that looks like. You're not insane, so don't date like an insane person. Date like a positive person who always wants to make things better, not worse.
- **Do understand that gender differences are not character defects.** Don't get into disputes where you're basically saying that he should act like a woman. That's why you have girlfriends.
- **Do realize your hormones are not reliable.** They've gotten you into trouble in the past, and they may get you into trouble in the future. The sexiest, most attractive man is not necessarily the best choice for you.
- **Do be available.** This means you need to check your e-mail, voice mail, etc., and respond. Indicate to him that you have time in your life to put into a relationship.
- **Do practice saying no.** First to a mirror, then move up to sales calls, then someone you really trust not to leave you, and then whenever you really mean it. And if you aren't timely, permit yourself to go back and say, "I'm sorry but I hadn't checked my schedule. I won't be able to help you or go with after all."

- **Do develop your communication abilities.** If you need to be a better listener, practice listening. If you need to be more self-revealing, practice expressing yourself more. You can't feel loved if you don't feel comprehended. And you can't be comprehended if you are unable to tell him who you are.
- **Do count on some negatives from anyone you're in a relationship with.** Deal with them as straightforwardly and as quickly as possible. Ignore the ones you can.
- **Do be assertive in letting him know you would like to go out or go out again.** This could mean calling to say you had a wonderful time or sending a note. But genuine and expressed enthusiasm toward him usually works equally well.
- **Do remember that some of the people who make excellent candidates for mates are not the ones with the fanciest footwork.** Some people who are really, really great on dates are well oiled by all the dates they've had. Also, the man who is more invested in commitment is sometimes a bit clumsier than the guy with nothing to lose.
- **Do realize that part of courtship is being willing to see his flaws so you'll know if you can love him, flaws and all.** He is flawed. You are flawed. We are all flawed. There is no perfect person or perfect relationship, so don't dash off as soon as you're disappointed. Ride through it to find out if it settles down into a doesn't-matter compartment, or if the two of you can resolve the difficulty.
- **Do be genuine.** Know yourself and act accordingly.
- **Do carry business cards with you so you can make yourself known, and easy to find!** Giving out a business card could help your business but it also is an excellent and subtle way of saying "I definitely want you to call me if you're interested."
- **Do ask questions.** It's a good way to get to know him and find out if he is open and a good communicator.

- **Do be prepared for rejection—it happens. Get really good at handling it.** Move on and find the person who does want to be with you. You may have already experienced pain and sadness after being left and lived to see the day you were thinking, "Thank you, thank you, thank you for dumping me." When the abandonment waves have passed, you sometimes realize that being left by him was a lucky break.

- **Do be enthusiastic if you want to see him again.** "I've had a nice time—thank you," is inadequate. Be excited. Be elated. Let your eyes drift lingeringly around his face and shoulders and smile with your eyes as well as your mouth.

- **Do keep the conversation positive.** No one wants to date a Debbie Downer. And if he does, you don't want to meet him.

- **Do give back, whether it's time, money, or thoughtfulness.** This can include calling back to ask if his sore throat is gone, whether the deal came through at work, or if he had a safe trip.

- **Do send articles that pertained to topics you discussed on your date.** It's a great way to remain in communication.

- **Do entertain in your own home on the third or fourth date—if it's presentable.** If not, entertain at a friend's or relative's home. The object is to demonstrate your skill at making things happen, and preferably to demonstrate your domestic competence on your own turf. You don't have to be overwhelmingly domestically competent, but get dishes out of the sink, and make spaces available for sitting. If you're at home, clean it. Repair glaring faults. Put out flowers. Have music he'd like to hear playing. If you have friends or relatives whom you feel sure would be liked by your date, invite them over. Turn off the phones, or at least the ringer. Give your date your attention.

- **Do discuss sex before it becomes an issue.** After is too late. Make sure you're in agreement about what it means.

- **Do seriously assess intentions between the fifth and tenth date.** You want someone who's communicating comfort with increased intimacy, someone who's interested in the long term. If he's truly uninterested, then say good-bye. If he does have marriage on his mind, you don't need to rush it. But keep the year in mind. By the time four seasons have passed, most people have decided if they want to marry or not.
- **Do focus on being able to have a good time by yourself.** If you rely on your date for all of your happiness and fun, you'll soon start to be miserable when he's not around, which only acts to lay the groundwork for a very unfulfilling relationship for you both.
- **Do admire and respect the person you're choosing.** Also, admire and respect yourself.
- **Do be willing to touch and be touched.** Lovemaking and all forms of physical touch are an area that is very important for you two to be on the same page. Most relationship counselors would say couples' problems are usually about sex, money, or love, and usually in that order.
- **Do know the facts about each other so there aren't any terribly big surprises.** No, this doesn't mean that you should put all of your flaws on the table on the first date, but if you have three children and four ex husbands, he needs to know that within six to eight dates—just be positive about what you have and what you've learned.

The point is to be yourself, have fun and to always work toward something positive. When you do, dating will be more fun, and everything that follows will be healthier and more productive.

Kick the Rules to the Curb

As you move forward, remember that rules are meant to be broken. If you have shared adoration, respect and an ability to communicate, most dating "rules" don't necessarily apply because they're already being adhered to without much thought. But for most couples, getting to that point takes a little tweaking in one area or another. Keep yourself in check and your partner in mind, and everyone will be happier.

Chapter 8
Be a Smart Shopper

Myth: I'll never find the right person.
Truth: With eyes wide open and dedication, I can recognize and keep the right person.

Now that you have a goal in mind, and a good idea of how to go about achieving it within your time frame, it's time to shop. Unlike the past, when you may have just been winging it, this time you won't go shopping blindly. You are going to be an ultra-savvy, educated consumer who knows what she wants in a man and isn't afraid to go after it with both hands—or to walk away if it's just not happening. With your goal of getting married or being in a committed relationship in a year, you don't have time to be a fantasy chaser or a time waster. It's time to meet your man.

> ## Love Notes
> *Either you feel great about yourself when you're with someone, or he's not the man for you. No exceptions to the rule.*

Try It On

In order to be a great shopper, you must take your time. You're not bargain shopping or running into a store and desperately grabbing something that you know you'll only wear once. You need time for comparison-shopping and for some in-depth analysis, time to try out and try on the person you're with.

When you try on a dress, it's a good fit or it's not. While dating isn't quite so instantaneous, you should have a similar idea about whether or not a man is the right fit after only a few dates. You may have to look at him from a few different angles, see what kind of wiggle room you have—he'll have to be flexible, stable, and sane. He'll also need to be some kind of adorable, attractive, and/or fun—and you must feel happy when he is near you.

> ## Love Notes
> Don't marry without believing the man right in front of you is 100 percent lovable, livable, and likable.

Take a few minutes to go back and recheck your Spouse Shopping List to be sure you are of sound mind and judgment, and feel free to search for affirmation from one or two of the wisest people you know. But keep in mind that if anyone is going to help you shop, their taste level has to match yours. The people around you need to share your vision of what you want to have and be on your side about having it—and that means that their view of whom they would choose for you is put aside.

See the Person in Front of You

You are on a mission to find the best person for your life for the rest of your life. That means that the man you are shopping for should, right now, be the type of person you want to marry. Too many times women say, "I thought he'd change once we were married," or "I thought our problems would be resolved after he committed." Perhaps the number-one dating fallacy is that marriage will change people. It might, but it may not be for the better. Look at the man you eventually select on an "as is" basis with a no-return policy attached. And before you begin dating exclusively, he should be most of the way there. After all, a piece of paper isn't going to make a cheater faithful. A ring isn't going to make an irresponsible person into someone to lean on, and a promise of commitment certainly isn't going to make a nondemonstrative person tell you day in and day out that he loves you.

The only way to stop wasting time or chasing fantasies is to focus on the person you see in front of you, not on what you hope that person might eventually become. You might be so eager to meet your soul mate that you think you're seeing him behind every bush or in every bar, but it just doesn't work that way. Get a clear idea of the guy (or guys) you're dating; don't just look for someone who will play a role in the lifestyle you want. When a woman is trying too hard to believe this is the one, she starts filling in details that are not there, trying to make him into what she wants him to be. She keeps fluffing him up as they go along. She has a built-in automatic excuse maker for him because she doesn't want to find out he isn't marriage material. Sadly, many of these stories end with some version of, "I made you up, didn't I?"

> ## Love Notes
> *Unconditional love means that your love and theirs is not for what either of you do but for who you are.*

LOVE STORIES: DEANA

Deana, a smart woman who usually had great street sense, "kind of had a feeling" when she went out with Samuel, a charismatic, sexy director of marketing, who explained to her that he was "almost separated." He and his wife still lived together, but he assured her that his spouse didn't mind if he went ahead and started dating. This red flag should have been visible in a total blackout, but charmed into believing that Samuel was her dream man, Deana let all thoughts of her Spouse Shopping List fly right out the window. She was swept away and riding the high.

Deana, like many women, was in complete love denial. While claiming to be on a straight path to true love, she willingly, happily, but foolishly took a major detour. In Deana's case, the predictable happened. With professions of "I am nearly in love with you" (now doesn't this have a ring similar to "almost separated"?), Mr. In Between, with tears in his eyes, announced that his wife was causing trouble for his children and he had to give up Deana. With Samuel out of the picture—and after a brief period of mourning—Deana swore off married, separated, and just-out-of-a-relationship-but-I'm-over-it men, and dated only men who were actually available. In fact, she moved this criteria to the top of her Spouse Shopping List.

Ask Tough Questions

Within six dates, you should know the answers to some tough questions about your potential mate:

- "Is marriage one of your goals?"
- "Do you want to have children?"
- "What are you looking for in a mate?"

If your man has not answered these questions in so many words, you might need to be more direct. If this is the case, try saying something like, "Don't get too carried away or flattered, this is not a proposal, but I want to know if, in general, you are marriage minded or are looking for a committed relationship." Some would find this level of specificity shocking or abnormal, and it is in the sense that it is unusual for women to be so confidently and clearly forthcoming about their future. This is no way close to a proposal of any kind or a testimonial about your being interested in him, in particular. You just don't want to find yourself wasting time with an avowed playboy, and it's okay to say that. All you want is to know that the two of you agree on what you both want in the future—even if you don't know at this point if the two of you have one together. He should be forthright with you, too; when men really want to get married, they are looking for a date rather than a bunch of dates, and they typically don't mind saying so.

It's important to communicate your concerns from a position of power, however, and not one of desperation, or even love. If you ask him if he wants to get married in a very desperate way, chances are, he'll read it as, "You will marry me, won't you?" Asking that way doesn't make you seem like marriage material. Instead, it's a turnoff and the answer will likely be no. Just keep in mind that this question isn't about the two of you personally as a couple. It's about your individual mind-sets—whether you see eye-to-eye on big issues.

> ## Love Notes
> *Don't bet on a horse that's*
> *not in the race.*

Still, actions speak louder than words; while some men will say they're not interested or they don't know if they're interested, you might want to give them a little wiggle room. There are many men out there who vow never to marry and they stick to this idea until the day they fall in love. You should know by now whether or not he is ready to eat out of your hand. In case of faulty instincts, you must find a friend who has good ones (male friends with no romantic interest in you are usually better than females at knowing if a guy is not into you), or buy some instinct in the form of an experienced therapist/counselor. Ask yourself: Does your guy look at you like he's won the lottery? Is he rearranging his life in even the tiniest way to have you in it? Does he care about you and the people in your life? Does he show you his stuff by presenting himself as a good catch? Is he at least somewhat more interested in you than himself? (This last one is the difference between a husband and a player.) If so, you know that you're on the right track.

> ## Love Notes
> *Remember that you are the shopper, and you have consumer power. You're the one making the choice.*

Do the Grunt Work

Like buying a house or car, there will be some grunt work involved before you find your keeper. In fact, there will be much, much more, because unlike a house or car, you're not finding a spouse only to trade him or resell. The grunt work is good, though, because you really don't need to be in a state of total glow all the time. You need to do a few things he wants to do that you don't want to do, and he'll have to do some things that you love that he won't. There needs to be some pleasure in pleasing or helping the other person.

Before committing to someone, you need to know a whole lot more about him than his ability to be good on a date. Real life, after all, is made up of more than candlelight and roses. Is your man good with women, or good with you? You want to make sure you're not with one of those men whose fifth date with you was identical to his fifth date with everyone else; professional charmers are lost without their stage set. So, early in the dating cycle, suggest some things that are your special interest and a bit off stage for romance, such as:

- Ask him to help you move a piece of furniture or put something together. This will show you how helpful or patient he is.
- Take him to a boring but obligatory wedding or work-related event. If you still have the time of your life, that's a good sign. If he stands around complaining about everything, he'll complain about even some of the good things down the line.
- If you're outdoorsy, suggest the two of you visit a local farm and pick food for your dinner and then cook it together. This will give you a sense of whether or not he's flexible and easy to work with.
- Do nothing together, like running errands or just reading the paper. Being busy is one of the ways couples put distance between them. The key is, can you be not-busy with someone? Are mundane things more enjoyable because he is around to do them with you?

If you have fun doing everything *and* nothing with your new mate, you're on the right track.

When to Consult Your List

At the end of Chapter 2, you hid your Spouse Shopping List as you began to date, which allowed you to approach the dating world as someone who was out there with her heart open, zealously making an effort to have a good time and making sure that everyone who is on a date with her is having a good time. However, you're not out there to entertain the world. You're trying men on, and one of the best ways to do that is to jump on into it and experience the person.

Within six dates with a man whose goals are in alignment with yours (which you will know, because you've asked the tough questions), you should refer back to your Spouse Shopping List. You may find that there were some things you thought you cared about, but this man has more than you dreamed of in your most important categories, so you can be a bit more negotiable that you thought. Still, you need to look back to make sure you're not so swept away by one trait (particularly if it is something you didn't get enough of in your last relationship) that you're willing to sweep away what you—of single, sound mind and body—decided you wanted.

At this six-date point, thoughts of your date should be positive. If you're constantly seeing what's wrong with him this early on, you are on the wrong road. It's not that you won't be annoyed, occasionally—you might be. But in that case, the question is: is it something you can let go, or want to let go, or something you bring up and they respond positively and can change? However, if you're busy crossing things out on the old shopping list, watch out. This person may be great and wonderful, but you want someone great and wonderful in the way that fits you. There are many terrific people who just don't share your values, attitude, and outlook. In the beginning, lust may override many of those concerns, but in the long run, they will matter; when it comes right down to it, even those things that seem superficial—like activity level or social level—aren't. For example, one person's idea that friends drop in anytime they want to could be the other person's worst nightmare in the house they share. In fact, overall attitude toward people is huge and can be picked up right away. Keep in mind that the way a man treats the waiter is probably very similar to the way he'll ultimately treat you. Your Spouse Shopping List helps protect you from a con; maybe not a con who will steal all of your money—but one who will steal your heart.

LOVE STORIES: HARRIET

Harriet was recently divorced from a pretty uncaring man and she was now desperately in love with a man twenty-five years younger than herself. He had picked her up at a Sunday school class and had been living with her for almost a year but was not interested in marrying her. He was basically just enjoying being with someone very attractive and generous whom he had wrapped around his little finger.

Soon, Harriet realized that coming from a cold-blooded marriage, she was just so happy to feel again that she didn't recognize herself for the doormat she had become. She didn't want to give up the first fun and passion she had felt in decades, but with this new realism, she was better prepared when her man finally left her. Harriet had learned that he was hardly the keeper she thought he was but just couldn't let go. He cut her losses for her.

> ## Love Notes
> *Whenever the pain in a relationship outweighs the pleasure, it is probably time to move on.*

Recognize a Keeper

People often ask how they can recognize a non-keeper before they end up throwing away years of their life. All you have to do is reference the Keeper versus Not a Keeper chart, which sets out basic qualities and areas of agreement—such as trustworthiness and spiritual compatibility—that are required in any successful relationship. You will also be alerted to any serious red flags that signal disaster like intolerance, chronic anger, and lying. It's easy to be blinded by lust, desire, and the pursuit of a romantic ideal rather than love, respect, and appreciation. This chart will force you to drag some logic back into the equation.

KEEPER VERSUS NOT A KEEPER CHART

Keeper	Not a Keeper
Trustworthy (and you are not just being blithe; anyone could trust them)	Has sexual problems you can't live with
Generous and not to a fault	Intolerant (it may be of other people now, but it will be of you in the future)
Communicative	Chronically angry and argues with no need for resolution
Has a sense of humor you enjoy or the lack of one you can live with	Addicted (if you can't tolerate them when they get worse, and they will)
Understanding of you (and they'll ask for information when they don't understand)	Has problems he is not currently solving
Respectful and kind	A manipulator who keeps you feeling sorry for him
Agrees with you about children, family, religion, spirituality, money, sex, friends, leisure time activities, houseguests, and household chores	Has eccentricities about money and hygiene that don't match yours
Holds compatible life goals	A liar
Pleases you	A taker
Shares difficulties	A nonlistener
Is lovable	A stingy communicator
Is spiritually compatible	Doesn't understand you
Will be influenced by you	Someone self-centered
Supports you in your decisions	No shared values

The truth is, when you have a keeper, you usually know it. The same goes for non-keepers. Unfortunately, you may have a harder time admitting to yourself that people are non-keepers. Consult this list when you need some help with that decision.

What to Do with a Non-Keeper

Don't spend too much time in a relationship you know isn't going anywhere just because you don't want to go through the trouble or pain of ending it. Yes, breaking up is often hard to do, but there are tactful and appropriate ways to end relationships that don't involve excuses or lies. And you owe both of you the opportunity to find a mate.

People always ask "What do you say" to end a relationship, because it seems like the most horrible thing in the world. You just have to remind yourself that you're not going to totally destroy a guy's life by leaving after a few dates. There are ways to say no politely. Just be as flattering as possible, while still being honest. Find a phrase that you feel comfortable with. For example:

- "I don't think we have a lot in common."
- "I don't want to go out again, but I thank you for (the dinner, the time, etc.)."
- "I find you a very delightful conversationalist, but I don't see a future together."

In any case, you should end the relationship gently but firmly and move on. Remember, as we discussed in Chapter 7, with every relationship you end, you're one step closer to the one that will last.

For a relationship of any depth or caring, honest, practical, and kind communication can be of great benefit to both parties when a breakup occurs. But avoid lengthy, in-depth analysis. You don't have time to work on every breakup as though you were in couple's therapy. If it has been a relationship of many months and some depth, then they may very well feel you owe them some explanation and details. If you feel that way, too, you can simply be honest. Try one of the following breakup lines by letter, e-mail, phone, or in person to soften the blow:

- "I believe we have different goals. You seem more interested in remaining single or keeping on dating, and I feel more inclined to put time into a relationship that will lead to marriage."
- "I have enjoyed our conversations and the time we spent together, but I don't feel that we have a future, so I want to end our dating at this point."

When you're going through the breakup, realize that when people say, "I don't understand," they usually mean, "I don't like it." And if yelling or character assassination occurs, quit immediately. At that point, everyone's learning curve is going downhill rapidly. Nothing is being gained. Just walk away and begin your search anew.

> ## Love Notes
> *You don't have to get to "What about no don't you understand?" Harsh breakups are usually unnecessary. Saying good-bye can be handled with grace and style.*

Keeping a Keeper

Once you've decided someone is a keeper, you want to make sure he knows it, and that you keep it in mind all the time. You can turn a keeper into a non-keeper by picking on the very things you thought were so wonderful, so remember the big stuff. Keep your checklist with you to remember all of the reasons he's a keeper. No one's perfect, and when his flaws show, you can go back and remind yourself that one small thing that gets on your nerves is not as important as all the reasons you decided to keep him.

LOVE STORIES: ANNABETH

Annabeth had her keeper but wasn't doing a good job of keeping him. J.T. had a goodhearted attitude and was genuinely happy. Annabeth, a perfectionist, appreciated his happy-go-lucky ways and was grateful but could not leave more than well enough alone. She began picking at the teeny-weeny dark side that goes with his personality type. For example, she praised J.T. for his generosity, but harped on how much he did for others. She enjoyed the fun he brought into her life, but chided him for not having more serious pursuits. Annabeth did care and did see how her criticisms hurt and puzzled him. The "you are so wonderful but now let me tell you how you should change" routine was cutting into their love and making them both miserable. She reassessed his value to her and realized before it was too late that her perfectionism was what needed the overhaul, not the man she had chosen.

Take the Good, Take the Bad

It would be difficult to define the intricate complexities of even one person in a book, but what you could call "the personality at large" generally falls into a group of people with similar characteristics. That doesn't mean that everyone fits into just one category, or that a category that is compatible with yours should be a blueprint for your future mate. But you should have a basic understanding of your personality type(s) and the personality type(s) of the people you will date.

Once you know where you fit in (and can understand your own makeup) you'll have an easier time articulating what it is you want and need out of a mate and a relationship. Your partner wants to be understood, and so do you, so it's important to know each others' personality types and the good and bad that come along with each. Like life, different personalities have ups and downs. While not an excuse for negative behavior, knowing your partner's personality type can help you better understand and accept his reaction to certain events or challenges. There are all sorts of personality assessments people can take. Knowledge as to what type of a personality you're dealing with can be used effectively in dating to know something about the other person and how best to relate to him. These types are found in books, magazines, online, and in sessions with therapists, but here are four that were originally developed based for sales training:

Doer

A "Doer" is outgoing and task-oriented. He needs challenges, and he needs to be in control of every situation. Doers have to make a concerted effort to notice other people who aren't on their same path, and they often have blinders on, so people around them often feel and can be neglected. To relate to a doer, you have to get on their agenda. You have to set dates with them and be very definite about what you're looking for from them. You might be attracted to the doer for his outgoing personality, but down the road you may feel neglected when he's working on a big project.

Expressive

An expressive personality type belongs to someone who is people-oriented, outgoing, and wants to be popular. These are the people who get so on a roll that they forget they're not the only person in the relationship. They're very attractive, so supporters are particularly drawn to them, but they can end up being an audience for a lifetime. Expressives need to regularly remind themselves that others might actually have something to say, too. To relate to an expressive, you need to speak up because they will assume you would if you wanted to.

Amiable

An amiable personality type belongs to someone who is usually reserved and steady; this guy wants to please. They want security and to be appreciated. They're all about team effort, but they are more of a follower than a leader. This is a common personality type. In relationships, they're the ones who won't speak up, then end up with a bag of resentment and hurt feelings. Amiables have to try to speak up before they get irritated or angry. To connect with them, you must be able to appreciate that they will please you if you tell them what you want, and you have to urge them to communicate.

Analytic

An analytic personality type belongs to someone who is cautious and competent; this guy wants answers and consistency. They are great in business situations but difficult in relationships, if you expect spontaneous responses. Analytics should practice more risky behavior than they are used to. It will make them lively and more fun. To relate to an analytic, learn to patiently wait for answers, because they have to think long and hard about their responses.

> **Love Notes**
> *Other pastures really can be greener.*
> *Get out of your usual playing field.*

Just as it would be great to buy houses that don't require repair and cars that don't break down, it would be great to only date people you might marry. But you can't have that—and if you could, dating would be pretty boring. However, you can know what you want and you should always have the right attitude so you're not making dating decisions that are based on grumpiness and fear. Focus on opening yourself up so you can present the best picture of you to the best possible person for you to marry.

Being a smart shopper isn't about picking someone perfect, it's about picking someone who's perfect for where you are in your life right now, and where you will go (together) in the future.

Chapter 9

Twelve-Month Timetable

Myth: If it's right, it will just happen.
Truth: You make your own reality. If it's right, you helped make it. Your job now is to keep it that way.

Many women complain that their relationships just don't go anywhere; they just idle along in neutral. They get into a relationship and things are good, but then little progress seems to be made toward their marriage goal. This is where the Twelve-Month Action Plan really comes into play. In this twelve-month plan, you'll learn what you need to do to go get into the relationship, and then what you need to do to make the relationship grow and thrive, till death do you part. While everyone's relationship won't adhere to this precise time table, you should pay attention to the developmental check points that should occur in every healthy relationship, like spending time with each other's friends and family, becoming completely open and honest, and declaring your commitment. Skipping any of these steps completely is like never learning how to read, and then expecting, all of a sudden, to be a published writer. In life and love, all along the way, you have to do the prep work required at one point to successfully get to the next step.

Month 1: Maximize Opportunities to Get to Know Each Other

The first month of a new relationship is fun and exciting, and it's the time to get to know each other by asking lots of questions, attending many events together, and meeting each other's friends. Go to lots of events and parties to get a sense of how your date acts around others.

When you're with him, do you feel like you're the most beautiful woman in the world? You should! Whether it is your hair, eyes, face, intelligence, or soul, you should feel beautiful to him, and not just because this is the time you will be on your best behavior, and will be making your effort to look your best; insecurities and excitement make people work extra hard in the first month. Make sure that you feel good when you're with him, and when you're not. You should both be excited during this time, and you should feel each other's excitement. If you're feeling blown off and ignored, ask yourself if it's your own insecurities or if maybe he's not as excited about you as you are about him.

If you're both clearly enjoying the courtship, enjoy this time, but not so much that you lose sight of what's important: your plan to meet and marry the dream mate for you. Recheck your Spouse Shopping List at some point during the first month to see if your new prospect has the qualities that you've decided you want in a mate and to be sure that he's not just charming you with his good looks, attentiveness, and great dates. If he's not what you had in mind when you created your Spouse Shopping List, re-evaluate your choice to make sure you aren't just trying to turn this person into some made-up version of what it is you're really looking for. If you are, move on to the next one quickly.

Month 2: Spend Time in Each Other's Homes

Now's the time to get a picture of how your potential mate lives while also offering a realistic, yet positive, portrayal of your own lifestyle.

By the second month, you have a good sense of your new mate, but spending time in his home will give you a much better picture of how he really lives. So work toward a combination of true representation yet savvy marketing on your own domestic front. Yes, you have to reveal that your apartment might be small and cramped. But you can also make sure that it looks warm and inviting.

Make Room in Your Life, Make Room in Your Home

If you bring a man to your house and you only have a place setting for one, room for only one toothbrush in the bathroom, no extra closet space, etc., he's going to have a hard time seeing how and where he'll fit into your life. Even the tiniest spaces can be accommodating for two people. It doesn't mean the two of you will live there together forever, or even that you'll ever live there together. But you need to demonstrate that you have room for him in your life by making room for him in your home, even if it seems early. And by all means, if you have a twin bed, do something about that *right now*. Having a twin bed indicates that you don't ever want to share your bed, and that's the opposite message you want to be sending.

Your home will be one of the places your relationship grows and develops over the next few months, so make sure that it, like you, is relationship ready. There are a few small adjustments you can do right now to make your home more appealing for a pair:

- Make sure your dining room table or eating area can accommodate at least two.
- Have a bedside table on both sides of your bed, and ensure that at least one is clear of clutter.
- Have more than one pillow on your bed.
- Don't have your toiletries covering all the space on the bathroom counter.

- Even if you don't empty one out completely, clear out some drawers or cabinets in your bathroom and bedroom to mentally prepare for the space his things may need in the future.
- Keep his favorite foods or drinks in your kitchen. This one is the most important. While the stomach isn't necessarily the pathway to a man's heart, all men do to be fed.

When it comes to men's homes, things are a little different. While it would be unfair to say that all men are messy and are terrible decorators, the truth is that many are not going to have the level of caring you have or exactly compatible tastes. It's probably not a bad idea to get over an excess of green leather couches, a wagon-wheel coffee table, or brown dishes. Like clothing, home decor is often an area that's very much up for discussion. Don't go so far as to take throw pillows or lace curtains over in the first month—that's too intrusive—but while helping him clean up before you have mutual friends over for the first time, you may start offering suggestions and helping him find a better home for that mysterious stack of seemingly important receipts piling up in the bathroom.

> **Love Notes**
> *You need to know the emotional price to know if you can afford to pay the bill.*

Month 3: Reality Check

The third month is the time for you to discover what is really important to the person you are dating. By this time, you're past the new-couple stage, and should know each other well enough to do little things to make the other person feel important and cared for. Concentrate on finding out how your potential mate likes to be treated and what his needs are (physically, emotionally, and other), and determine whether you are willing to meet them. At the same time, make sure your own needs are being recognized and fulfilled. It's important that you teach your date how to treat you well through requests, not through demands. Unsure of how to do it? Try suggestions like these:

- "I know it was hard for you, but I felt really connected to you when you shared your feelings with me last night. I hope that you will continue to share with me. When you do, I feel closer."
- "When you rubbed my back last week, it melted my stress away. Sometimes I really need your touch to relax at the end of a hard work week."
- "I know it's a little out of your way, but I'd really like it if you could pick me up before our date on Saturday."
- "I love to get flowers from you, and the colors you chose last week were beautiful."
- "Your compliments mean the world to me."
- Even if he is sparse with praise or gifts, catch him at being good then gush.

Avoid explaining why you want what you want. Just bottom-line state your desire and use the excess words to tell him he makes you happy or appreciative by giving you what you need.

> ### Love Notes
> *A cyber boyfriend is not better than no boyfriend at all. Either he is making time for face time with you or he is not that eager to connect.*

This is also the time to make sure that the two of you share the same life goals, or at least know that your life goals are compatible. Know what he wants to accomplish in three years and where he wants to live, as well as what makes him the most proud about himself. If you think you will go back to school, or want children, or will be going on girl trips regularly, the time to say so is now. You should only continue the relationship if all the important choices are shared or supported by both of you. Remember, your dream mate is out there somewhere. If the guy you're with isn't the right one, then hold out for the one you want.

LOVE STORIES: GLORIA

Gloria and Bob had been together for a few months. They had a very good physical relationship, but anytime they broached a serious topic—political, religious, or any other area where there could be an incompatibility—Gloria backed off. She just wanted to believe that Bob was perfect. He avoided taking her to his place, being accessible, or introducing her to friends, but she made excuses for him: Her place was probably more comfortable anyway. He was busy. Being alone was nice. When Bob all of a sudden broke up with her, her parting line to him was, "I made you up, didn't I?" And she had. Gloria should have been charting the relationship to see if it had been progressing. Turns out, the relationship wasn't going anywhere, but Bob sure was.

> ### Love Notes
> *Listen with your eyes. Behavior is truer than words.*

Month 4: Determine Emotional and Sexual Compatibility

For most couples who choose to have sex before marriage, the fourth month is the time they begin to be comfortable in each others' beds. While sex isn't the most important part of a relationship, it is a very important one and can serve as a barometer for how other things are going in the relationship. By now, there are a few questions you should be able to ask yourself and the answers should be positive:

- Do you feel good about yourself in the other person's presence?
- Are you both respected and respectful?
- Is your sexual relationship mutually satisfying in both frequency and choreography?

If you have decided to postpone sex, feel free to discuss your needs and desires openly and thoroughly. If you're postponing sex, it is a red flag if only one person is having problems sticking to the decision. Being on the same page sexually and emotionally keeps a connection in the relationship. In my experience, the old adage, "No man ever left his wife for a better cook" is true.

LOVE STORIES: MARGARITE

Margarite came to my office after a year and a half of post-divorce dating. She had had sex in her marriage but never good sex and she was determined to have fun. She said her motto was to keep dating multiple men until she was engaged. Not a bad idea at all, but bedding down all of them was getting a little confusing for her and not the best idea for health and well-being in general.

Coming from the sexual desert that was her marriage, she was understandably thirsty and seeking affirmation of her own desirability. She was also wearing out. Her present problem was that she was not getting anywhere in her desire to find a mate and she was beginning to feel depressed.

Her biggest problem in reaching her goal may be the biggest problem for anyone. We tend to run to the man who can make up for what the last man couldn't or wouldn't give us. Fine, but the problem is that in being so grateful to have this need finally met, we can be blind to the flaws in the new man—seeing him as a savior when he is actually a stop-gap, thereby ending up with yet another relationship deficit—just a different one. Margarite was also hiding from the vulnerability of loving just one man behind her three men. She had put too much of her self-esteem in her ex's pocket and was not sure she wouldn't do the same thing again.

After six months of building self-esteem and understanding her part in choosing and staying with the wrong man, she chose one of her contenders and has stayed with him. He seems suitable, but she is using the trust-but-verify method of learning more, trusting more, then staying at that new level of trust. It is only after she feels there are no ill consequences of the greater closeness that she will be ready to forge ahead.

> ## Love Notes
> *Beautifully planned first dates don't necessarily predict great relationships, but a man with an imagination wears well.*

Month 5: Do Things Together

In the fifth month, take a long, hard look at how the two of you function as a couple by doing a wide range of activities together. Make sure the things you do run the gamut from traveling together to volunteering together, taking courses to going on double dates, hosting joint parties, running errands, exercising (which is particularly good since you'll be sharing an endorphin high), going shopping, planning future events, and of course, sharing boring, everyday chores. You need to make sure that you enjoy your potential dream mate during run-of-the-mill activities. Anyone can appear attractive and appealing over a great meal by candlelight, but a dream mate will also be enjoyable when doing yard work! By month five, the initial butterflies may be gone (if you ever had them in the first place) and if you still want to do things, as well as nothing, together, you're on the right path—especially if you can do them with compassion and understanding.

Month 6: Get Personal

At this point, you're halfway through a year with your partner and you should feel confident that you know and accept his background, emotions, work patterns, social patterns, and goals. If, by the sixth month, you haven't accepted those things, it might be a good time to either re-evaluate your relationship, or figure out why you can't be more accepting and how you can. This is also a good time to explore your feelings about the influential people in his life, including family members. Think thrice if you can't accept and respect those people, and particularly if they live in the same town or visit often.

> ### Love Notes
> *Don't give your in-laws-to-be a chance to look like mourners at your wedding. Start now to iron out difficulties or, better yet, let your husband-to-be do the ironing.*

If you have conflicts with your future mother-in-law, take her out to lunch and find common ground in the fact that you both love her son. If your partner has children and his ex-wife is a problem, then that is a challenge you're going to have to make a hard decision about. If you think it's an issue that will just go away with time, you could be waiting forever. So make very sure that it's something you're willing to deal with as a team. You should also make sure you believe he is doing all he can do so you won't end up picking on him later with your complaints about her.

But no matter what issues you have to deal with, remember that when you get married, you rarely marry just the person—you get a whole family and sometimes a village. Be sure you're ready.

Month 7: Determine Spiritual Compatibility

Determining spiritual compatibility doesn't mean agreeing to go to the same church service together every week; it means feeling a spiritual connection to your mate. More than being in love with love, a spiritual connection is devotion, a sense that this is a good and desirable person, and loving your connection to him. A dream mate is a huge investment of emotions and time. Without this sense of spiritual compatibility, at some point you are likely to think your mate isn't worth the investment.

> **Love Notes**
> *Be sure that your love is for the person and not a romantic ideal.*

By this seventh month, which is simply an outside for your instincts to be operative, if you're in a dream-mate-quality relationship, you will feel the bond. You should feel drawn to him, just talking to him should be a pleasurable experience, and you should feel confident that you could enjoy each other indefinitely.

Now that you've realized that your spiritual connection is intact, you should take a good look at your sex life (if you've made the decision to have sex). Sex is a large part of a good relationship, but it can also keep people in relationships that they consider undesirable by all other measures. These people stay for the high, not for the person. Lust can be a part of your connection but in a playful sense. What you need to continue is knowing your sex life is based on the depth of love and like and respect.

As hard as it may be, before you marry, try to do without sex for even a small period of time. Share a small space. Take a trip. Rely on his decisions and spend a day doing only what he wants to do. Ask him to spend a day doing only what you want to do, but keep sex off the table. If your feelings for him haven't changed after your short break, chances are your spiritual connection is intact.

Month 8: Conflict Resolution

Couples succeed or fail based on their ability to handle conflict and change. In the eighth month, you should be able to let your partner know when you're angry or sad without melodrama or excessive pain for him or you. You should be able to ask for reasonable changes in the relationship without eliciting a disproportionate response. Pay particular attention to how he handles change and adversity. Can you offer each other comfort and unconditional support? Alternately, can you both express love and joy in a satisfying way?

> **Love Notes**
> *The content of the fight is less important than your process for resolving it.*

You may have had some fights at this point. If so, when the fight was over, did you both feel satisfied, listened to, respected? We'll talk more about resolving conflicts in the chapters to come, but realize that conflict is a part of any relationship. If you and your partner can resolve it quickly and painlessly, learn from it, and move on with a better understanding of each other, then you're on the right track. If not, it's never too late to realize something isn't working and jump track.

Month 9: Hide Nothing

By the ninth month, absolute unbridled honesty is essential. Now is the time to make sure you've disclosed everything from health problems and debts to family difficulties and skeletons in the closet. And don't hold back on self-revelation because you think he might disapprove. Likewise, make sure you feel confident that he has done the same. Ask every question you can think of. It's difficult to make a well-informed decision about someone when all the cards aren't on the table. Not every single past error needs to be revealed, but if something weighs heavy on your mind or affects the present or the future, it needs to be brought to light. At this point, you and your partner should discuss all aspects of your future lives together—good and bad.

LOVE STORIES: CECELIA

Cecelia had bad credit. Having grown up in a difficult home, she lied about her age at seventeen to get a credit card, which she used to move away from home. Between loans and credit, by the time she graduated from college, she had racked up nearly $50,000 in debt. Over the years, she tried to fix her credit and worked hard to pay off the debt, but it always seemed to snowball. By the time she met Tyler, when they were both twenty-eight, she owed various agencies and companies more than $60,000.

Within two months of dating, Cecelia knew she wanted to be with Tyler long-term. But she also knew he had immaculate credit. Ashamed of her money troubles, she never told him about her much-less-than-perfect credit score and level of indebtedness. She was worried that Tyler wouldn't want to marry someone whose bad credit rating could affect his own.

Eight months into their relationship, they were planning a trip together, but she kept stretching out talking about it. When a cheap airfare to one of the destinations they were discussing popped up, Tyler asked Cecelia to book the plane tickets, telling her he would reimburse her for his. But she didn't have a credit card to book them with and wouldn't have the money until payday. When she said she couldn't buy the tickets and Tyler asked her why, Cecelia broke down in tears and confessed what she'd been hiding. To her surprise, he hugged her, told her he'd book and pay for both plane tickets, and said that he admired her hard work toward fixing her credit. He told her that with his knowledge, he could help her consolidate her debt and bring the light at the end of the tunnel closer. Yes, it was her problem, but he would help her solve it. While he said he wished she would have told him sooner, he was glad to know what he was getting into ahead of time. Still, he was happy to help her if it meant spending the rest of his life with the woman he loved.

Love Notes

Hiding creates shame, which makes a flaw seem even larger. Bad credit is not ax murder.

Month 10: Soul Mates

Whether you like the term or not, a soul mate speaks to something deep within you. There's trust and intimate intertwinement. By the tenth month, you and your partner should be best friends, and you should feel a closeness that is unmatched by any other relationship. The two of you should know that you want some of the same things out of life. But some soul mates are made, not born, and intimacy is something that can grow if the roots are there. People become soul mates by sharing their souls, and if they match, they're soul mates— that's why hiding nothing and baring yourself to your partner is so incredibly important.

LOVE STORIES: RUTHIE

At a dinner party, Harry was proudly saying that he and his new girlfriend had met online and matched on all dimensions. Amidst the "Oh, how sweet's," the longtime married woman Ruthie beside him looked across at her husband and said, "Ralph and I don't match on any dimension, we argue a lot, and we are probably incompatible, but we adore each other." And that, too, is a soul-mate connection.

Not everyone would want to clone their relationship, but those two couldn't imagine not going through life arm in arm. Not every relationship looks pretty on the outside, and it doesn't need to. It is hard to assess what two people feel. You can match or not match. All that matters in that you agree on it. Soul mates know it's their experience that matters, not having an attractive wrapper.

Month 11: Marriage Is Mutual

By the eleventh month, whether or not you have a ring on your finger or have made a lifetime commitment, you and your partner should have similar feelings on all issues, and every topic ranging from children and money to friendships, family relationships, sex, love, and household management should be resolved. Make sure that you are very clear about the life you want before you say "I do." Do you want to work? Stay home? Be certain that you are able to speak freely with your mate on any topic and that you believe that he will tell you the bad truths as well as the good. If a wedding is in the works, then you should be so eagerly anticipating marriage that you are ready to run down that aisle. If something about the wedding is causing problems, it may be hinting at what may be wrong with the marriage in the years to come.

LOVE STORIES: AARTI

Aarti's wedding was referred to as a coronation, not a wedding. Her mother and wedding planner became her constant companions, and the groom, Ameet, a distant relative. He was literally schooled in dancing, protocol, and speech giving, and he was directed to use the stylist of their choosing for every outfit he was to wear to the twelve prewedding events, rehearsal dinner, wedding reception, and a brunch the morning after the wedding, before they could leave on the honeymoon. Ameet had only two complaints: that he missed Aarti tremendously, and that he had to come up with ten groomsmen to match her ten bridesmaids. His plea of not knowing ten men (and possibly needing to advertise in the paper for them) was hardly heard, let alone discussed.

Aarti and Ameet survived this magnificent affair without lingering resentment or worry that the fact that Aarti had, for a time, seemed wedded to her mother—not him—might continue. Ameet knew he trusted Aarti completely, and that fact was what brought them through the wedding planning process—but Ameet was still probably the most relieved man in the world to make it to the honeymoon.

> ### Love Notes
> *Make sure you're focusing on the forest:
> the marriage rather than the wedding,
> which is the proverbial trees.*

Marriage Is Mutual Checklist

Discuss everything on the list below before deciding to spend the rest of your life with someone. While you don't have to agree on everything (like religion and politics), you at least have to agree to disagree and be respectful. When it comes to more important matters, like when or if to have children and where you will live, you must reach some sense of understanding and compromise before moving forward with marriage.

Your Premarital Discussion Checklist
- Money
- Credit, and how and when to use it
- Whether to rent or buy a home
- Relocating
- How many children you want to have
- When to have children
- Whether or not you'll work if/when you have children
- Time spent on work, hobbies, or other individual activities
- Religion
- Politics
- Household duties
- Your responsibilities (financial or other) toward your family members
- Sexual frequency, interest level, and style
- Attitude toward family and friends
- Level and type of social involvement

If there are issues on this list that you and your partner haven't yet discussed, now is the time to sit down, chat about those issues, and see where both you and your partner stand on the issues at hand.

Month 12: This Is Your Marriage

After nearly a year together, you are experiencing what marriage will be like. Whether or not you've tied the knot by this point, your life as it is by month twelve (or after you've taken all the steps leading up to this point) is pretty close to what it will be like for the rest of your lives together, but it doesn't mean there isn't room for improvement. Are you happy, satisfied, and content with what you have now? If you aren't, then change it now before you marry. What you see now is what you will get. Things aren't going to change just because you have a marriage license and wedding bands. If you can't live with your partner's behavior and attitudes now, either make the necessary changes or make your exit. Doubts require action.

If you are happy with your life as is, you've discussed the big things, your partner meets your most basic requirements on your Spouse Shopping List, and you are thrilled to be marrying him and confident in his ability to be a great husband for you, then you are good to go. How exciting! Remember this feeling, and let it remind you of why you chose this person in the first place. Your work isn't through. Marriage is a full-time job, but the best is yet to come.

{ PART 3 }
THE ROAD TO
HAPPILY EVER AFTER

Now the fun begins. You've found your keeper and are making certain that the choice you make is wonderful and lasting, that your heart and brain have a united front when you decide to fully commit. From this point forward you cannot lose. You've developed your abilities to shop, catch, and keep. And whether you're in a committed relationship already, or determined to have one in the next few months, you're now living in Real Man Land—a world full of appropriate, loving, sane men who would make good husbands. You have learned how to be an appropriate, loving, sane woman who would make a good wife. Here you'll learn how to go forward and maximize your learning and loving for the rest of your life.

Chapter 10

The Big Decision

Myth: Common interests predict a good marriage.
Truth: Your own interests will be even more interesting with someone you love, trust, and respect to go home to every night.

After you've found and spent a significant amount of time with your dream mate, the next logical step is marriage or a committed partnership. It's easy to get caught up in the idea of a wedding and everything that comes along with it, but you can't forget the most important part: marriage and a lifetime commitment to your partner, who should by now be your lover (at least in the larger sense of the word) and best friend. You and he must completely trust and respect each other, have shared your goals and desires, and love each other unconditionally. But before you make the big decision, you need to be sure that not only is he the best possible man for you, but that you're willing to put in whatever it takes to make it succeed—and that he is as well.

Unconditional Love

Are you capable of loving unconditionally? And are you sure you know what that really means? Unconditional love is the ability and willingness to love someone regardless of their actions or beliefs. Many people tell their children they love them unconditionally, but can you say the same thing to your partner? Will you love him just the same when he messes up or fails? Will you love him and support him regardless of any conditions, even those with which you do not agree?

Children test their parents by asking, "But would you still love me if I killed someone or flunked out of school and couldn't get a job?" While the questions you ask yourself about your lover need not be that extreme, ask yourself if there are any conditions under which you would stop loving him. If there are, you do not have unconditional love. And if you want to marry this man, you need to figure out a way to love him unconditionally. Quickly. The best way to develop your ability is to discipline yourself to think loving thoughts, re-formulate your perspective on behaviors you don't like, and giving the benefit of the doubt.

> ### Love Notes
> *You need to love the whole person with your whole heart—and your brain.*

Mutuality

Before you decide to enter into marriage, you need to start thinking in terms of mutual interest on a daily basis. Up until you began dating your dream mate, your life probably revolved mostly around you. And unless you have children or are taking care of someone, that's okay! have! But now that you're considering spending the rest of your life with someone, your way of thinking needs to change in order for your marriage to be successful. No longer will the world revolve around just you; it will revolve around you and your mate as a couple, a team, a partnership. It's you and him, together against the world if need be. You're making decisions that are right for the both of you—and keep in mind that from this point forward, you might not always be the one making the decisions.

When it comes to the bigger things in life, you'll have to consult your partner, hear his point of view, consider it, and make a joint decision based on both of your thoughts and feelings. But when it comes to even your everyday decisions, they need to be made in the context of the consequence for the other person. Even the most mundane things can affect your mate. For example, if you know he's going to have dinner waiting for you when you get home from work, you probably wouldn't have a big snack at 3 P.M. like you might if you were on your own and could decide to skip dinner. You *should* still keep your best interests in mind, but pay attention to that little voice inside your head that asks, "How would this affect him?"

> ## Love Notes
> Remember what your parents (should have) told you: the world doesn't revolve around you.

LOVE STORIES: JILL

When Jill began dating Mike, he was attracted to her independence. She had a great group of friends, could go on vacation without a tearful good-bye or checking in every ten minutes, and she had varied interests that he found interesting as well. However, after things got serious, Jill's independence didn't wane, not even a bit. Once, after they were living together, Jill booked a plane ticket to visit a friend for a New York weekend without checking the date with Mike to see if he had plans for that weekend and only told him at the last minute. When Mike conveyed his annoyance, Jill thought he was unreasonable. He told her he was beginning to feel like an afterthought and needed to be a part of her decisions, or at least be informed with enough time to set plans of his own. Her independence was part of what had attracted him to her, but it was also what was keeping them from moving forward in their relationship. There were a few more incidents like the plane ticket, but Mike gave her time and Jill started being more considerate. What she found was that it wasn't annoying to think about his wishes, and it didn't hold her back—it just made her feel closer to the man whom she eventually married.

Trust

In healthy relationships with mutual trust, couples will be comfortable away from each other for short periods of time, and possibly extended periods of time with lots of check-ins. In fact, keeping up with some of your own interests will be key to your happiness and the health of your relationship. However, too much self-interest can be troublesome. Some couples have such separate interests that over time, they have less and less to talk about, which means their relationships have less and less connective tissue. Also, the busiest couples, even if they do their socializing together, are going to run into problems. An intimate relationship requires some downtime and some alone time. The key is to find the balance of time together versus time apart that works for your relationship. This will vary from person to person and relationship to relationship, but be sure to allow him the individual time he needs, and take yours, too. You'll know that you've found a good balance if you savor time together, but have enough trust in the relationship that either one of you could be absent in pursuit of a project, sport, or anything else without worry from the other. In an ideal situation, you'll be okay when you're apart, but still miss him.

LOVE STORIES: JANEY

Janey, a single client of mine who wanted to be in a relationship as soon as possible, was extremely thoughtful about what she wanted in her marriage and had very definite ideas about building trust. When Janey first wrote me, she said: "I want to try to understand my new partner and learn all of his likes, dislikes, desires, and preferences. I also want to keep my mind clear and free of confusion as it relates to all issues affecting us. I will try to bring up any concern that starts to weigh on my mind. I hate carrying around worrisome issues, so I want to always try to bring them up and really listen to his reaction. I consider myself flexible and willing to adjust, but I believe anything buried and avoided will eventually surface again and become a more difficult issue. I know I tend to avoid troublesome conversations, so this will be an area where I have to push past my comfort zone in order for my mate to know and trust me."

An obviously sincere and thoughtful woman, Janey was way ahead on any relationship curve by having a pregame plan for getting close by initiating open and honest communication.

Honesty

You can't have trust without honesty. It's as simple as that. If you're hiding something, it's going to hurt you—and your relationship—in the long run. Blurting out startling information after the wedding makes a spouse feel justifiably duped, so make sure all big revelations are confessed somewhere before or during month nine, so your man has time to assess the situation and decide if he can handle the information. And keep in mind that whatever you might be afraid to say is potentially less hurtful than withholding something from your mate. Secrets are omissions, and anything less than the whole truth is a lie.

Now, being honest doesn't have to mean making a laundry list of every terrible thing you've ever done, or showing your partner every embarrassing picture of you. But it might mean telling him you used to be overweight, so he'll have a better understanding of your being a little obsessive about what you eat and when. Or it might mean sharing a painful sexual experience that could explain your less than free and open sex life and help him realize that gentleness might be the only ticket with you. But whatever you have or haven't done, if your partner loves you unconditionally, the revelation won't matter in the long run. Allow him some time to be taken aback and some space to think and digest what you've told him, but have enough faith in yourself and your relationship to know he will continue to love you and accept you for who you are today. If you don't have any large skeletons in your closet, just be honest about the little things as they come up.

Love Notes

The truth—as inconvenient as it can sometimes be—usually comes out one way or another. Wouldn't you rather it be on your terms?

Respect

If you don't have respect for your partner, and vice versa, your relationship is doomed. Respect is what will keep things civil when you're having a disagreement, in private or in public. Respect is what will demonstrate to your children that even when the fire is temporarily burned out, relationships can still be successful. Respect is what every human being desires, and because it is sometimes hard to come by out in the real world, it's something every person wants, needs, and deserves at home. That means not taking out your daily frustrations on your partner. The second he becomes your punching bag—emotional, verbal, or otherwise—it's no longer you two together against the world; it's you versus him. Always keep in mind what you love about your partner, and if you've had a rough day, count to ten, meditate, or stop off at the gym before you walk in the door. You may want and need to talk to your mate—just don't do it until you can share your woes without hitting him over the head with them.

Your mate wants you to be responsible, self-respecting, nurturing, and a friend. He wants to feel like you have worth and expect quality in the person you marry. Don't be a doormat, and don't turn him into one. A true partnership is not bonded servitude. It is adoration and mutual respect.

Respecting your partner also means accepting and respecting his background, whether he grew up in a trailer park or he was a trust-fund kid who never had to work for anything until he graduated college or if he never graduated college. If he has done things in previous relationships that he regrets, respecting him means not using those things against him in your current arguments. If he has a sordid past, respecting him means not bringing it up to put him down. Respecting your partner means loving and believing in who he is today, and not punishing him for anything he may or may not have done before you were together.

> ## Love Notes
> *You should be proud to call your mate your partner or husband, and treat him well both in public and behind closed doors.*

Goals

Shared goals are paramount to the success of a relationship. This isn't to say you shouldn't have your own individual goals, because you should. But you should also support your partner's individual goals just as he should support yours. However, if you don't want the same big things out of life, your paths may split at some point. If one of your goals is to save a large amount of money and have a large house before retiring, and you're dating a person who's content in his hourly wage job, you may find trouble down the road. If you want to have six children, and he wants one, that could be a problem. If you want to go back to school, you should have a serious discussion about what that would mean for your partner who would be taking on more of the day-to-day expenses and chores while you do. If he wants to build the house the two of you will live in, you should be prepared to get your hands dirty and maybe even live in a trailer on site for a while. Luckily, a big part of courting is sharing your hopes, dreams, and goals, so by now you should have a good idea of what the other person wants out of life. Still, now is a good time to review those goals and make sure that you're both on the same path romantically and realistically.

> ## Love Notes
> It's easier to reach for the stars when you have someone to hold the ladder.

Desires

People aren't always as forthcoming about their desires as they are about their goals, but desires are just as important. You have all kinds of desires—physical, financial, emotional, social, geographical—and so does your partner. Are yours similar? Or at least compatible? While you don't have to have all of the same desires, they shouldn't contradict each other. So make sure you talk about your desires now so you're not caught off guard by a seemingly strange sexual fetish, or a sudden desire to move to Australia. Some of the more important desires to discuss are below:

Sex

For the most part, by the time people marry, they have set their sexual pattern. But whether or not you and your partner have had sex, it's important to talk about your intent for the future. Do you want sex three times a week? One time a week? Does your future husband want it every day? Whatever the case may be, talk about it now, so you both have a realistic expectation of the other person's sexual needs and how they will be met.

Names

When you marry, will you take your husband's name? If you haven't considered it, you should now. For some, a woman taking the man's name is an antiquated, pointless tradition that just causes more headaches and paperwork in the long run. For others, it's a symbolic glue that holds a family together. Maybe you both want to create a new, hyphenated name. You and your partner may have differing views on this, especially if you plan to have children. Just make sure it's something you talk about before you are pronounced "Mr. and Mrs."

Geography

If you want to live in Paris at some point in your life, and you'll be miserable on your deathbed if you never make it there, tell your partner now. While you don't need to map our your entire life in detail at this point, you do need to know whether or not you'll be marrying a fellow adventurer, or someone who wants to keep his roots right where they are. On the other hand, you may be perfectly happy staying put, and he may be considering a move. Whatever you want, make sure you talk about it before one of you ends up disgruntled.

Friends

While it may seem inconsequential now, ask your partner how much time he wants to spend with his friends, and be honest about how much time you want to spend with yours. This could mean the difference between a romantic vacation for two or a vacation for four or more. Both are fine, if it's what you both want. Just be honest about it from the get-go so you are clear about what would be comfortable for you both. There aren't any rules, other than not going past the point that would leave one partner feeling abandoned or lonely or the other controlled.

Children

Before you marry, you and your partner should be in agreement about whether or not you want to have children and if so how many and when. If children will play a role in your life in any capacity, take the time to have a very serious talk about the role they and grandchildren will play in your life. While children don't get a vote, by now they should know you're marrying someone who will love and respect them as a stepparent, and that they are expected to be respectful and courteous in return. Talk about how your children will be a part of your life down the road. Do you believe in financial gifts or assistance? If you want to help your son buy his first house, that's something your husband should know and if not be in agreement of, at least accept. If your grown grandchild gets laid off of her job and asks to move in, will your new husband protest? How will remaining income be distributed in your will or wills?

Go back through the "Marriage Is Mutual" checklist at the end of Chapter 9 and make sure you've discussed every item on that list that's applicable to your relationship. No question is too minor or too bizarre. It is having the right to know and agree or not agree before marriage that people care about. Once married, saying no gets a little more complicated.

> **Love Notes**
> *In most cases, you won't get what you want unless you ask for it.*

Reality

There's a reason marriage vows include the disclaimer "for better or worse." Sometimes marriage is hard and it can't be pretty every minute. That's why it's important to have a real grasp on reality. Will you love your husband if he loses his entire life savings in the stock market, his legs in a terrible accident, or his beautiful head of hair to genetics? If the answer to all of those questions isn't a resounding "yes," you're not ready for the reality of marriage. By deciding to enter into a lifelong partnership with someone, you're agreeing to take on everything life throws his way right along with him. And vice versa. This doesn't mean you should stand idly by and put up with abusive or addictive behaviors or not speak out if his way of dealing with problems is to sink into untreated, unmedicated depression. But it does mean that, within reason, you should be ready to face the world together, fielding whatever curve balls life may throw at either or both of you. You should absolutely know by now if he is good at life or a trouble magnet. You need a guy who will do as much as he can to make your world wonderful—and you need to be prepared to reciprocate in kind.

> ## Love Notes
> *Life's ups and downs are more manageable and less painful with someone you love by your side.*

While relationships require some compromise, you shouldn't feel like you're compromising yourself or settling when you get married. Your spouse should be a great addition to your life, not a drag, an embarrassment, or a project. The joy that comes at the time of an engagement is an indication that both you and your partner feel like you're getting a good deal. And you both should be. Does the idea of spending the rest of your life with this person feel right? Are you elated? Do you look forward to kissing him for the rest of your life? If you're not sure, go back and revisit the Keeper versus Not a Keeper chart in Chapter 8. You need to be confident that your mate is a keeper and that you are a winner for having him. Also, take the following quiz to make sure you're ready for marriage.

CHECK YOUR DECISION TO MARRY

Answer "yes" or "no" to the following questions to determine whether or not you are truly ready for marriage.

1. Are you capable of unconditional love?
2. Are your partner's needs and satisfaction as important to you as your own?
3. Do you absolutely trust and are you completely trusted?
4. Have all "skeletons in the closet" been revealed?
5. Are you respectful of each other's backgrounds?
6. Are your goals and dreams the same or ones your spouse will support?
7. Have you expressed and heard all desires and expectations, all hopes and fantasies?
8. Can you both hear and take complaints from the other?
9. Have you considered the "or worse"?
10. Do both of you feel that you are getting a great deal?

If you answered yes, without hesitation, to all of the questions, you are ready to marry your dream mate, and he is ready to marry you. Congratulations! But remember, your work doesn't stop here; it's only the beginning of the most important job you'll ever have.

Love Notes

When shopping for clothing or men, don't buy it if it doesn't make you feel great.

Cohabitation

For some people, moving in together is part of the big commitment. For others, especially younger couples, it's a step toward a bigger commitment. Studies have historically shown that couples who lived together before marriage had slightly less of a chance of remaining married, but more and more, people are moving in together because it's a financial advantage and makes sense. Living together is not necessary. It may hurt, it may help, or it may be a time when both or one of you is auditioning because you do want to get married.

LOVE STORIES: JANELLE

Janelle met John just as he was finishing up a master's degree at a university a few miles from her house. Immediately, the two hit it off. From the very beginning, neither was nervous about expressing excitement over the relationship, and it seemed that the trust and communication that had been missing from all of Janelle's previous relationships were there in abundance with John. She felt wonderful when she was around John, and wonderful about her relationship when she wasn't. So, when the semester ended and John's lease was up, Janelle didn't have to think too hard about asking him to move in. She did give it some thought, including "This could be crazy," but she and John talked openly and honestly about the pros and cons of moving in so soon. In the end, they decided they were both incredibly committed to and happy in the relationship, and that moving in together could only make them closer. Plus, Janelle joked to me later, "If it's not going to work out, this is a great way to find out sooner than later." Two years later, they're now engaged and as happy living together (though in a new house) as they were the day John moved into Janelle's apartment. Part of their success was a true willingness to let the relationship fail if that seemed to be the truth of the matter. Too many live-in couples make the mistake of being on unnaturally good behavior, auditioning for the big commitment.

The Proposal

So, you've made the decision you want to marry this man, and you believe he feels the same way. Then what? Women often ask if they should just sit around waiting for a marriage proposal. Most of the time the answer is yes—wait for the proposal. Men don't usually like to be usurped. The proposal might not happen exactly on your time frame, but if you have the confidence it will happen, it's best to wait for him to take the lead. However, if you have a notorious procrastinator, or someone who is painfully shy, it's okay to drop a few hints. Start with assurances, like, "You make me so happy and here's why." Build up to some version of, "You're the type of man I've always dreamed of being with," or even, "You're the type of man I'd be proud to call my own." If that still doesn't work, you can always say something like, "I can't wait to be married to you someday." If he turns bright red and vomits, rethink your decision. If you're sure he's meant for you and that he really wants to marry you, consider proposing to him. This may not work for, say, an older, more traditional man, but if you're dating a guy a bit more nonconformist, go for it.

LOVE STORIES: GEENA

Geena, a lawyer, sent a written four-page proposal to Maxim, her boyfriend of a year and a half. She detailed the pros and cons of a potential partnership, listing questions he might have, suggestions for date and location of ceremony, and presenting a compelling argument of the feasibility of a union between them. Maxim, after the initial shock, enthusiastically said "yes!" At their wedding, he eloquently announced during the ceremony that there was nothing in the world he ever wanted more than to marry her, that he was going to ask her a month later, but that by her asking, she had given him the gift of making his dream come true.

Whenever the decision to marry comes, and however the engagement develops, you should know you're okay on your own, but be thrilled at the prospect of a life enhanced with your dream mate. Also, you should feel confident in your decision because you have discussed your wants, needs, desires and fears with your partner, but it's important to realize that the conversation doesn't stop here. How you continue to communicate is of extreme importance.

Chapter 11

Connection and Communication

Myth: My partner knows I love him without me having to say it.
Truth: My partner needs to feel my love for him with everything I say and do.

It's a given: connection and communication are the keys to a healthy marriage. Even the greatest relationships suffer when either fails. Both members of a couple must possess the courage to express what they want and who they really are. You need to be able to speak up for yourself and create an environment in which your partner can speak freely and honestly as well. If you don't feel understood, you won't feel loved, and the same goes for your partner. It's that simple.

At the same time, you have to communicate with tact; there's a reason people sometimes shoot the messenger. Bearers of bad news are often irritating. Read on to learn how to communicate effectively without nagging or being confrontational and take a look at some important guidelines for communication and what your partner needs to feel loved.

Communicate Effectively and Deliberately

It's important that as you get comfortable in your relationship, you don't get lax when communicating with your mate. Unfortunately it's easy to do. The chart below gives you some tips on the right ways (and the wrong ways!) to convey messages and the correct responses to give in order to keep the peace.

COMMUNICATION ALTERNATIVES CHART

Never Say	Do Say	A Good Response
"What's your problem?" (Very cranky)	"Is there something you want to discuss or change?"	"I want your help." Or, "I would like to tell you," using a neutral tone of voice.
"You don't listen to me..." or "You fly off the handle when I try to speak." (You are fanning the flame.)	"I care about talking to you and appreciate that you will listen to me."	"I want to hear what you have to say and will be calm or ask to table the discussion until I am able to communicate better."
"Calm down." (Guaranteed: they'll be more upset than ever.)	"Something must have happened, can you tell me?"	"I don't know that I can right now but would you hold me, listen, or ____."
"You don't care about my feelings..." (Puts them on the defensive and they will be exonerating themselves instead of taking care of you.)	"I know that you love me but when you ____, I feel ___, and prefer that we could___. Is that okay with you?"	"I must not have shown you as well as I could, but I do care. Please give me another chance."
"Use your brain" or "Be logical." (Patronizing)	"I'm not being clear. Please tell me what you did hear, and then I'll explain it better."	"I think you mean___— just tell me what I've missed."
"You are an idiot, heartless, a nag, etc." (Creates distance. Character assassination is not good foreplay.)	"I appreciate your awareness, concern, and caring about our relationship. Could we start over?"	When words fail, a logical, heartfelt, and succinct e-mail might be in order.
Anything in a lecturing, complaining, or whining tone. (It's pompous, manipulative, and demotivating.)	Hold hands, make eye contact, keep it in the now, and speak as though you are addressing a peer.	"What is it that I could do for you?" Act friendlier than you feel.
"Always or never..." (Even the worst of us gets it right sometimes.)	"Would you do me a favor?" Then state your *present* complaint—no past, no future.	"That is something I can correct." Do not defend yourself.
"I can't talk to you about anything important." And then cry, sulk, rage, or withdraw. (Not fair)	State what you want or need without making them bad for not having already delivered it.	"Whenever you are ready, I want to hear how to please you."

Conveying your true feelings is important, but how your convey them is just as important. Make sure that when you communicate, you are not adding extra hurt or complications to the problem at hand. The point is to move forward with a better understanding after every uncomfortable conversation.

Fighting

In a perfect world, couples would never fight. But you don't live in a perfect world, and people often feel misunderstood, neglected, insecure, and any number of other emotions that can lead to fights and disagreements. That doesn't mean your relationship is headed for doom and gloom, and it doesn't necessarily mean you are any less connected. Fighting, or arguing, can even be healthy for a relationship if it's done respectfully and you both come out of it with a better understanding of the other person when the conflict is resolved.

Some couples go at it more often and find it's part of their sense of passion. They might just be more emotional, and that works for them. No matter who you are, fighting stops working or being constructive when you break the rules. If one or both of you begin making cruel remarks, then you're just creating garbage. You can be colorful, but never be cruel. If you've said something so terrible about your partner that he'll never be able to forget, you've done damage. It's important to keep a cool enough head about you when fighting to remember these simple Fight Rules:

- Be very specific when you introduce your complaint.
- State what change would satisfy your complaints.
- Get feedback to make sure they've heard you.
- Deal with only one issue at a time; get one issue resolved before moving onto another.
- Be prepared to compromise.
- Never assume; ask what each other's feelings are.

Be especially mindful to not finish sentences or try to "help" your partner in a fight. Don't help. You can and should restate what he's trying to communicate to you, but a fight is really not the time to put words into his mouth or tell him how he feels.

Love Notes
Telling people how they feel is insulting.

Agree on a Code of Behavior

In most relationships there's one person who's more verbal. If this is you, you might feel you have a partner who shuts down when arguments arise. This is good news and bad news. People need to be allowed to quit, but there are people who will always quit when there's conflict and will never approach or resolve the problem. If this sounds like your partner, go back and review the fight rules and write a few more of your own that apply specifically to your relationship. If you can agree on a code of behavior, it levels the playing field for the verbal and less-verbal players, and will make resolving a disagreement a bit easier. For example, you may reach a type of gentleman's agreement in which the one who is the talker has to learn to wait a bit to allow the person who may not be as quick at communicating to get his or her point across.

There are rules in teaching and journalism that say if you ask a question and really want an interaction, count to twenty before you go on. Invariably, at twenty, a student or interview subject will speak up. For a talker, twenty seconds of silence can be agony, and seems like the longest amount of time in the whole world, so counting it out in your head creates that balance between your normal rate of response and his. If, after twenty seconds, your partner doesn't answer, you can say, "Is there anything else?" If the problem hasn't been resolved, usually there is something else.

Create a Time Limit

For other couples, a good rule is putting a time limit on your arguments. Someone who avoids confrontation is often someone with limited focus, and a time limit helps them focus on the topic at hand. A time limit also helps the more verbal person to work on being succinct and get to the bottom line more quickly. Women can sometimes explain what they want, why they want it, when they first wanted it, and so on, with so much detail that their husbands are worn out before they've gotten around to saying what it is they really want. Try saying what you want, quickly, with no explanation of why you need it or why you should be getting what you are asking for. Then get the feedback. Maybe there's nothing more to say. It's important to not go on tangents, or you can lose the other person's interest, thus having less of a chance of receiving what you wanted.

Don't Dredge Up the Past

Yes, fights are often rooted in the past, but you can't fix the past, only the present. The worst thing you can do in a fight—other than physically or verbally attacking—is drag the past into it, and blame someone today for something he did a week, a year, or a month ago, virtually bringing up everything bad he's ever done. In transactional analysis, they call it throwing in the kitchen sink. It's opening the floodgates to something very bad, and that's destructive. Save the talks about the past for times when you're not fighting.

Listen, Listen, Listen

When you're working out a disagreement with your partner, be sure to give him your undivided attention, look him in the eye, and stayed rooted to the spot. If he can see that you're listening, he's most likely to be calm and to believe that you truly care about him and about what is being resolved. Even if he won't concede in whatever the argument is, he will at least walk away feeling heard.

When you argue, keep in mind that you might have to let go of one connection to maintain another more important one. Trying to communicate with someone while also talking on the phone or typing at the computer isn't only ineffective, it can be hurtful. When you're communicating with your partner, especially on the important issues that need resolving, make sure that's the only thing you're doing.

Don't Be Afraid to Go to Bed Mad

Contrary to popular belief, going to bed angry is not the worst thing in the world. Couples' fights often happen at night. Why? Sometimes it's because people are tired, which makes everything seem more dramatic. If you can go to sleep with a truce, or a pause, whatever it was you were fighting over may not seem so bad and sometimes not even memorable after you've slept on it and in the light of day.

Keep Connected

As important as communication is, without connection—touching, sensing, and giving what you have learned your spouse needs—a relationship just doesn't even exist. Connection is the all-important key component to a happy marriage. This Keeping Connected Book of Rules gives quick tips on how to maintain connection throughout your relationship. Refer to it often. In fact, write it down and keep it in your medicine cabinet, your desk at work, or anywhere else you might see it on a daily basis.

The Keeping Connected Book of Rules

- Sleep as naked and as close as you can.
- Always keep his strong points and what you love about him on your mind: positive regard is essential for a good attitude.
- Talk about him positively to others. If you must vent, do so only to your mate's biggest fan or your therapist.
- Be happy on your own: happiness is infectious.

- Stay tuned in to what goes on in his life and check in to see how things went—be a part of both the problem solving and the fun in his life and support him in what he wants.
- Show you know he is special by listening without interruption.
- Be the first and most profuse to compliment his accomplishments.
- Join your partner in some of his choices and be cheerful about it.
- Regularly clear the air: when something bothers you, speak up and suggest an alternate behavior. No one, but no one, reads minds.
- Make all of your communications kind. No excuses.
- Develop a sense of timing: bring up the harder issues when neither of you is tired, hungry, or troubled by outside pressures.
- Give the gift of gratitude and appreciation: let him know he is a success at making you happy.

There is a bright side to fighting and that is moving forward with a better understanding of each other. You and you partner are going to argue. Just make sure that when you do, the disagreements become opportunities to learn more about one another.

LOVE STORIES: ELIZABETH JANE

Jesse was a guy who knew how to keep a lady happy. He had three rules: 1) What the lady wants, the lady gets; 2) Spoil her, spoil her, spoil her; 3) When in doubt, refer to numbers 1 and 2.

One of this clever man's ideas was to make every day Valentine's Day with a card or e-mail or Post-It note daily. His mate, Elizabeth Jane, knew she'd find something somewhere but never knew what form or where she would find them. Jesse's notes could be written on a mirror, hidden in the pocket of her coat, or e-mailed at a precise time so it would be the first thing she saw when she sat down at her desk at work. A week's worth of notes included the following statements:

- "I always know the best is yet to come when I am with you."
- "You are the center of my life."
- "My challenge is to keep you in love with me for a lifetime."
- "In some prior life, I chuckled at the idea of soul mates; now I know I have found mine in you."
- "Sex based on love is two melting into one and waking up in heaven."
- "You are hot. You are beautiful. You have class. You entrance me."
- "I love kissing you, the way you smell, the way you dress, the way you undress, making you laugh."

Men have a lot to do with the success of a relationship, and Jesse is an example of a man who decides to be responsible for the romance level in his marriage and wins.

> ### Love Notes
> Note to self: keep his most loving messages and texts on your phone and reread and replay if ever you are feeling less than fully satisfied with him or whenever you want to smile.

Make Time to Make Love

At this point, if you have a sexual relationship, you may be thinking that making love is a given. But, unfortunately, over time, most couples stop making love with the frequency they did in the beginning. The longer you are together, the more obligations you have, and that usually lessens your opportunities to spend quality time alone together. Take every opportunity you can to make loving physical gestures toward each other even if it doesn't ultimately end in intercourse. If one or both of you is too tired for sex by the time you go to bed, go to bed earlier. And remember: you don't need to be in your bed to make love. Have sex on the weekends during the day on the living room floor or in the kitchen. If you're with lots of people, make love with your eyes. Steal glances across the room or touch each other under the table. You certainly don't need to be gratuitous about your public displays of affection, and grossing out the kids or dinner guests is not the goal—in fact, it's more fun when no one knows you're doing it.

Love Notes
Always take and make opportunities to connect intimately with your partner.

If you need to communicate to your partner that you desire more sex, try to do it in a nonverbal way first. You should know by now what it takes to get him interested, so just do it. And if you can focus on being a better and more generous lover, he's probably going to want love making more often, too. If he is pressuring you for more than you want, speak up in a gentle way with expressions of how attractive he is to you. Explain that his backing off a bit gives you room to desire him and keep that promise.

Kick the Kids Out of Bed

The family bed concept where the entire family slept together in one bed didn't last long, and here's why: It's terrible for your sex life and can get a bit weird as your children grow. It might bring a sense of connection to the entire family, but it tends to lessen the connection between parents. Unless you have a newborn who needs to be in your room, your kids belong in their own beds.

Also, feel free to take things a step further and put a lock on your bedroom door. Without one, having a comfortable, relaxing sex life is hard. You will always be nervous about your kids walking in, and you really don't want to risk traumatizing them or yourself. After all, what's sexy and relaxing about an image of the kids walking in and screaming every time you and your partner start to undress? You don't have to keep your kids out of your room at all times, and yes, having all the kids tumbling into bed on a Saturday morning can be fun, but make sure it's on your terms, when your bedroom door is unlocked.

> ## Love Notes
> *He may have to love your dog if he loves you, but he shouldn't have to sleep with it.*

Keep Your Pets Out, Too

Bonding over a pet you both love is great. But if one of you is bonding more with the pet than with the other person in the relationship, you have a problem. If you have a pet, does it bring you closer or keep you apart? If it's the latter, it doesn't mean the pet has to go, but reconsider its role in your life. Pets can come between couples literally and physically. Someone who is lavishing more attention on a pet than on a partner is likely avoiding intimacy in the relationship. In addition, some pets like to sleep right between their two owners, making it impossible for your and your partner to touch each other, and touching, sexual or not, is good for a marriage and good for your health. Luckily, dogs can be trained within a week to sleep in their own bed on the floor and cats adapt even more quickly and may care even less about sleeping with you than you care about sleeping with them. If you are both still sure you want the pet to sleep in the bed, train it to sleep at the foot of the bed, or on one side.

Do Things Together

Doing things together is a great way to be mutual, and just be together, deliberately. You and your partner probably do things together all the time: eat meals, pay the bills, watch TV, and clean the garage. But make sure you're taking time to do things together just for the sake of doing them, and not because they have to be done. Carve out some time to spend exclusively with your partner. Take a class together, like cooking, or painting; or exercise, nap, or read the same book. Share a sense of adventure by traveling together. Exercise or train for a race together. There's a special bonding that comes along with working out together because your endorphins kick in at the same time and you and your partner will share a natural high. You can get similar highs from sharing good food, laughter, socializing, learning, and volunteering. It really doesn't matter what you do; the point is to do it together.

Share a Calendar

Sharing a calendar is of utmost importance. So many fights start just because someone didn't have the right information.

He: *I didn't know about your great-aunt's birthday lunch.*
She: *Well, I told you.*
He: *Well, I must not have heard you.*
She: *You must not have been listening.*

This is precisely what a shared calendar can help prevent.

Sharing a calendar, either online or on paper, eliminates the gray area when it comes to social commitments. He can't be mad because he cooked a big dinner without looking at the calendar to know that you would be at spin class instead of the dinner table, and you can't be mad that he can't come to your last-minute work cocktail party because you already know he has a long-standing weekly softball game and the team counts on him. You can also keep track of when all of your bills are due, and anything else that's important to you as individuals and as a couple.

If you face incredible resistance to a shared calendar, send him an e-mail about everything that relates to a schedule. "Do you want to go to this party at Kyle's house, at 8 P.M. this Friday?" Or leave a note. If it's in written format, there's a better chance he'll remember. And he might even get so tired of keeping all of the e-mails straight he'll agree to keep a mutual calendar.

> ## Love Notes
> Sharing a calendar means upping the probability that neither of you will ever miss very important dates.

Enjoy Every Minute

If you are at a point where you are able to openly and honestly connect with your partner you've also reached a point where you're open and honest with yourself about who you are and what you need from life. Congratulations! You couldn't be in a better place and you couldn't have chosen a better person with whom to spend this next exciting chapter of your life. Enjoy every minute, even the less perfect ones. It is your enjoyment and respect of each other that will get you through more difficult times.

Chapter 12

Keep Love Alive

Myth: Love fades over time.
Truth: With emotional intelligence, dedication, education, deliberate intention, copious goodwill, a commitment to expressing the love you feel, and faith, love will continuously grow and thrive.

As you prepare to ride off into the sunset with your dream mate, it's important to remember that love involves some work. But it's so very worth it. Nothing in life is better than a marriage that works. But you need to keep your relationship moving forward with creative loving and effort. Stasis doesn't exist in a relationship, and if you don't work at keeping the love alive, things will start moving backward quickly. If you stopped working at your job, you'd probably lose it. The same thing goes for relationships. How can you keep your love alive now and in the years to come? Read on!

Stay on the Sunny Side

How you think may be more important than what you do or say, and a perpetual positive outlook is effective divorce prevention. If you're constantly negative, that's going to spill over into every aspect of your life. And if you're thinking about his flaws or any flaws in the relationship, chances are that your man will move away from you; men are especially intuitive in this regard. But if you think, "I am with this great, glorious, wonderful person," even if you don't say it, you'll motivate him, help him feel loved, and add fuel to your relationship.

Say Five Positives for Every Negative

It really is true that if you don't have anything nice to say, you shouldn't say anything at all. Love is fragile. Bring up problems only when you are able to handle them well—not in the middle of an argument, or when you're tired, hungry, or upset about something else. Nothing dampens a love relationship more than yelling, fault finding, and character assassination. Make a point of being kind and supportive and verbalizing your positive feelings. Gush, fawn, write memos, send carrier pigeons. It doesn't matter; just keep the flow of good loving going so that when negativity befalls you, you have a cushion of the good.

Kiss and Hug Every Day

Pecks don't count and neither do shoulder hugs where almost no other body parts touch. Skin-on-skin contact is good for your physical, as well as mental health. Remember those deep, meaningful kisses that made your pulse race and your heart flutter? Don't save those for the bedroom. Making them a daily part of your relationship keeps things loving and sensual and romantic. It doesn't matter if it's the most erotic, exciting thing; it just has to be a daily, intimate connection. Once you start adding pets or children to the equation, be sure that your mate is still getting his full share of hugging, stroking, sweetness, and caring.

Protect Your Romance from Overscheduling, In-Laws, Bosses, and Children

Make sure you have enough take-care-of-you time, as well as ample time to connect with your partner. You have to make a conscious effort to make room for yourself and for romance. Decide what you have to sacrifice to keep love alive. Being overly involved and committed to work, church, volunteer activities, hobbies, exercise or sports, the kids, your extended family, or friends is the way couples can create distance. Do have a full and rich life, but if your marriage is important to you, you need to give it the attention and emotion it needs to survive.

Love Even When You're Angry

Separate the person from the problem and try to get rid of your anger before you express it. Anger is only going to be destructive if you act on it without first getting a grip. Remember, no matter what's gone on, you still love him, he loves you, and whatever it is that is upsetting you was probably not done with the intention of upsetting you. Don't be afraid to state this before you get into dicey discussions with your guy. Words are devastating, and you're not arguing with someone you want left bloody and bruised. Sometimes you'll end up saying something when you're mad and your partner will remember it forever, not because he is unforgiving but because what you said was unforgettable. Anyone can forgive but if it's deeply hurtful, you can't erase it even if you try. Breathe, count to twenty, and remember that this is your dream mate. He's not perfect, and neither are you.

Act with Love

If something's not done with joy, it doesn't really count. Once you start doing things because you think you have to (whether it's making dinner or kissing your spouse), then you're moving toward resentment. That negative feeling comes across and turns giving and loving into tasks. Your mate will sense your lack of wholehearted willingness and may be somewhat uncomfortable and definitely less grateful. If you're begrudging or dreading, either find a way to put your heart in it or let your heart find another way to show love.

Talk at Least Twenty Uninterrupted Minutes a Day, All at Once

For some couples, this might be easy. For others, finding twenty uninterrupted, consecutive minutes every day is hard. Turn off your phones, the TV, the radio. Lock yourselves in the bedroom or the bathroom if you have to. Talk in the morning, the afternoon, or the evening after the kids have gone to bed. It's not important where you do it, or when you do it, but how you do it, and that you talk every day.

Make and Keep a Regular Date Night

Be very serious and deliberate about taking a once-a-week date night, or afternoon, or date morning. Decide on a time and take your date at the same time every week. If you don't feel like going out, no one says you can't stay in your pajamas, watch movies, and eat ice cream, as long as that time is uninterrupted and enjoyable for you both. Other people might get offended, or think it's weird, especially at first, but setting time apart to spend one-on-one with your partner is important for your bonding. Think of it as a job: unless you're deathly ill, or plan far in advance, you show up for your scheduled shift. Marriage may be the biggest adventure you'll ever have, so if you can't show up for the main event once a week, how do you plan to stay on the ride?

If somebody wants to do something during your scheduled date time, just say, "Sorry, that's when we're together." You might get some strange objections at first, but eventually, you will feel closer as a couple, and your friends will not ask during your appointed evening and be more respectful of the bond of your relationship.

De-Stress Your Married Life

In Chapter 5, we talked a lot about stress-proofing your dating life. Revisit that list, because many of those items can be applied to your committed relationship. The most important way to de-stress your married life, however, is to show your partner more love. And then show him even more. People feel less stressed if they feel more loved. All the while, remind yourself that you are a team and he has your best interests at heart. But don't forget to take some time to love yourself. You shouldn't expect your partner to be the source of your every joy, inspiration, and creative endeavor. Take the time to spoil yourself whether with a massage, exercise, or drinks with your most supportive girlfriends. But whatever you do, be sure to spoil your mental self as well as your physical self. And there are so many benefits to exercising together it bears repeating. When you exercise together, you share a natural high, and you can be relaxed together.

Have an Annual Review

People often think I'm joking when I say that marriage licenses should require continuing education, but I could not be more serious. Usually, people don't resort to couples' books or counseling until they have difficulty. But you should take the opportunity to be ahead of the game and prevent any slips before they become issues. To do so, an annual review of your marriage can be helpful. This review shouldn't be painful or something you dread. It should be an exciting time, and done with the idea that you're strengthening your relationship and making it better. If you dread an annual review of your partnership, something's going wrong and/or one of you is an unwilling participant.

Structure your review any way you'd like; if you want to do it stark naked over a glass of champagne, in a hotel room, or while you're on a bench in the park, that's okay. Just make it romantic and productive. It's really just a basic look at the state of your marriage and an opportunity to tell each other how well you are doing and what you specifically admire and appreciate about each other. If problems exist and can be resolved, do it. If they can't be resolved, agree to disagree. It should take less than two hours, but you're certainly not doing your relationship any harm by scheduling some extra time after the review to just hang out together and enjoy each other.

Share Your Goals

During your review make a list of the things that are important to you as individuals and as a couple. In a relationship, you often have to compromise time for jobs, children, or other family, but when you know that something is really important to your partner, it can change how you plan your time together and apart. Numerous studies have shown that people who write things down are more likely to get them done. Goals to write down include:

- **Long-term goals:** In all of the craziness of daily life, it's often easy to lose sight of the things that really matter. Keeping a list of what's most important to you both individually and as a couple can help make the important things your priority. Know what each of you want in one year, three, and five.
- **Places you'd like to visit:** Write down the places you'd like to visit together, and below each destination, list the action items it would take to get you there—money, learning a language (doing this together would be a great way to bond, by the way!), or scheduling a long-term babysitter.
- **Each other's goals:** Your partner might think of something for you that you would have underrated in yourself and not thought about. For example, you might see yourself as a not-so-good cook, and he might see your passion and talent without the self-critical goggles women tend to wear. He might set a goal for you to cook for a dinner party of twelve that you thought you couldn't handle, or he might have creative ideas about how you could increase revenue in your business. You might see by the little notes he writes you that he's an excellent writer, and encourage him to get a story published, or help him see how valuable he is and use that confidence to negotiate for something he wants but hasn't tried to attain.
- **Financial goals:** Talk about what you want out of life in the next five, ten, twenty years, and how you plan to get there. And also talk about what you want retirement to look like. How much is it going to cost to make your goals happen? Figure these things out now and keep a list of what you need to do to make them a reality. You may need a financial advisor or accountant another day, but for now just make a basic list and note the first steps to take.

When making goals, financial or otherwise, don't be afraid to ask your partner for his help in reaching them.

Exchange Valentines

I read a story about a fourth-grade teacher who had all of her students write down a list of everything they liked about their classmates. The students got the lists of what their peers liked about them, and it was amazing how much those lists affected the students. Many of them carried those accolades with them into adulthood and would reread them and feel a glow every time.

Do the same thing with your partner. Don't just say it; write it down. Write down everything you appreciate and everything you love about each other. Tell your partner what touched you most in the ways he expressed his love for you, and ask him to do the same. It's important to write these things down, because from year to year, people won't remember what they said, let alone what their spouse said.

Reflect on Challenges

Look back on problems you may have faced throughout the year. Discuss how you solved them, and what you could do better next time. Is there a way to improve your game plan in terms of process? Is there a way you need to pull together more as a couple? When discussing negatives, remember to always sandwich them in between positives. This isn't a time to fight. It's a time to reflect and plan for your future together. Brainstorm ideas of how you can get closer.

> **Love Notes**
> *Relationships flourish with common values and goals, open communication, emotional availability, and unconditional love.*

Also discuss annual events. Is there anything you or your partner would like to change about the way you do holidays or other celebrations? This is the time to discuss it, not when you have both families inviting you for Christmas or Passover.

The Love That Binds

Remember, love is what binds you but it's not the only thing that ties you together. Marriage is the most important job you will ever have so make sure you're giving it all of the attention that you can. Only then will you experience the true happiness that you deserve.

Afterword

Congratulations

You have kept on track and worked your way through this book. If you've taken the time to make positive changes in your life, you're either well on your way to finding your dream mate, or you already have.

If you're not there yet, go back and check every chapter month-by-month. Deal with issues of your past, de-clutter your mental and physical space, and go out two to three times a week. Do something every day that contributes to feeling good and reducing stress. Remember: feeling good means looking good! Flirt, review dating tips, and learn new social skills. Focus on what you want—not on what you don't yet have. If you've learned one thing from *Get Married This Year*, hopefully it's that changing your way of thinking will help you get what you want. Devote time to learning more about communication, love, and relationships. Make this lifelong learning.

If you have found your dream mate, continue to reference this book as much as you need to avoid possible pitfalls, keep your relationship stress level low, and communicate and connect effectively with your partner. Don't hide from yourself or your mate. Take a serious pledge to work on enhancement in your love match. No one can fight alone, but you can love alone, at least for a while if you need to get you both back to a place of mutuality and caring. Put your ability to love before all else. This will spill over into your parenting, friendships, and work. Love with your heart and your mind. Ask your mate how you can be a better partner—and gently explain how he can be better too.

By following all of the tips in this book, you should have made your own life better. Adding your dream mate to the mix is the icing on the cake. Having someone by your side and on your side is one of the best things you can create in life. Always remember to show him or tell him how much that means to you.

What to do after the "I do" is give much more than you did to get there. What was the bait that lured him into marriage? Whatever it was, he thinks it's tasty, and it is your responsibility to keep feeding it to him. Ultimately, being married isn't important. The fine art of being happily married is what truly matters.

This is not an end, it's a beginning. Enjoy the ride!

Index

Grunt work, 160–61
Guilt, retaining, 50–51

Happily ever after, 189, 227–28
Healthy tips, 78–81
Hiding nothing, 182–83
Honesty, 24–27, 182, 195–96
Honesty quiz, 26–27
Hugging, 220

Imagination, 111
In-law concerns, 179, 220
Information overload, 109
Intimacy, 103–4, 198, 214–16

"Keeper"
　Keeper Chart, 164
　keeping, 166–67
　recognizing, 163–67
Keeping love alive
　act with love, 221
　anger and, 221
　annual reviews, 223–26
　attitude and, 219–20
　communicating, 221–22
　date nights, 222
　hugging, 220
　kissing, 220, 221
　overscheduled lives, 220
　positive attitude, 219–20
　reducing stress, 222–23

　resentment and, 221
　time for romance, 220–22
Kissing, 201, 220, 221

Law of attraction, 75–76
Leadership role, 38
Learning new topics, 90
Life story, 10–11
Lifetime commitment, 191–205.
　See also Marriage commitment
Listening skills, 35–36, 59–60,
　90, 142, 211–12
Love
　annual review of, 223–26
　attitude and, 219–20
　communicating, 221–22
　keeping alive, 219–26
　making love, 214–16
　priority of, 227–28
　time for, 220–22
　unconditional love, 83, 124,
　　157, 191–92, 195, 225
Love blocks to avoid
　baggage, 51–52
　emotional clutter, 51–53
　fantasies about love, 57–59
　guilt, 50–51
　hoping, 48–50
　inability to listen, 59–60
　lack of self-awareness, 53
　negative attitudes, 55–56
　perfectionism, 55
　pet peeves, 61–62

About the Author

Janet Blair Page, PhD, has been a psychotherapist in private practice for over thirty years in New York City and Atlanta. For over twenty years, she taught "I Will Be Married in a Year" at Emory University's Evening at Emory, which was consistently one of the school's most successful courses. Dr. Page has been featured extensively in the *New York Times*, *Glamour* magazine, *New York* magazine, *Ladies' Home Journal*, and *Self* magazine. She has appeared on CNN, NBC, *The Early Show* on CBS, FOX, *Good Morning America*, *Sally Jesse Raphael*, *The Roseanne Show*, and *The Danny Show*. Dr. Page lives in Atlanta, Georgia. Visit her at *http://drjanetpage.com*.

2/12